THE GREEN-FINGERED GARDENER

kitchen gardens

THE GREEN-FINGERED GARDENER

kitchen gardens

the definitive step-by-step guide to growing vegetables, fruit and herbs

richard bird

southwater

This edition is published by Southwater

Southwater is an imprint of Anness Publishing Ltd
Hermes House, 88–89 Blackfriars Road, London SE1 8HA
tel. 020 7401 2077; fax 020 7633 9499
www.southwaterbooks.com; info@anness.com

© Anness Publishing Ltd 2001, 2004

UK agent: The Manning Partnership Ltd,
6 The Old Dairy, Melcombe Road, Bath BA2 3LR;
tel. 01225 478444; fax 01225 478440;
sales@manning-partnership.co.uk

UK distributor: Grantham Book Services Ltd, Isaac Newton Way, Alma Park Industrial Estate, Grantham, Lincs NG31 9SD;
tel. 01476 541080; fax 01476 541061; orders@gbs.tbs-ltd.co.uk

North American agent/distributor: National Book Network, 4501 Forbes Boulevard, Suite 200, Lanham, MD 20706;
tel. 301 459 3366; fax 301 429 5746; www.nbnbooks.com

Australian agent/distributor: Pan Macmillan Australia, Level 18, St Martins Tower, 31 Market St, Sydney, NSW 2000;
tel. 1300 135 113; fax 1300 135 103; customer.service@macmillan.com.au

New Zealand agent/distributor: David Bateman Ltd, 30 Tarndale Grove, Off Bush Road, Albany, Auckland;
tel. (09) 415 7664; fax (09) 415 8892

Publisher: Joanna Lorenz
Senior Editor: Caroline Davison
Editor: Emma Hardy
Photographer: Jonathan Buckley
Designers: Ruth Hope, Ian Sandom
Production Controller: Steve Lang
Illustrator: Liz Pepperell

Previously published as *Creating a Kitchen Garden*

1 3 5 7 9 10 8 6 4 2

PUBLISHERS' NOTE
In the United States, the burning of plants or bulbs
(if they are diseased, for example) is prohibited.

ACKNOWLEDGEMENTS
The Garden Picture Library: 6b (John Glover); 40t (Mayer/Le Scanff); 40b (Juliette Wade); 42 (Clay Perry);
45t (Mayer/Le Scanff); 46t (Michael Howes); 51b (Steven Wooster); 54 (Brigitte Thomas); 79t (Lamontagne).

The Harry Smith Collection: 6t; 24bl; 72t.

Jonathan Buckley: for the soil samples featured on page 40.

contents

introduction

ABOVE **Retaining a kitchen garden with dwarf box hedging is the ideal way to keep the area neat and tidy. Here, sunflowers add the perfect decorative touch to the garden.**

BELOW **These terracotta forcers are used to hurry vegetables such as rhubarb into growth. They also serve an ornamental purpose, dressing up what can be a dull vegetable plot.**

At the beginning of the 21st century it may seem something of an anachronism that people in the so-called civilized world should be growing their own vegetables. Not only are they readily available from supermarkets, but there is also so much else to do with our time. But take a look at people who do grow their own produce and you will usually find healthy, happy souls who enjoy good food – there's more to it than saving a little money.

In the days when spending a few pennies on seed saved much more at the greengrocers, growing vegetables used to be the cheap option, but this is no longer necessarily true, particularly if you include your own time in the equation.

People's reasons for growing vegetables and fruit vary widely, but nearly all vegetable gardeners would say that the crops you grow yourself are far superior to those you buy. There is, of course, an element of one-upmanship about this, but this is far from the whole story.

Above all, vegetables from your own garden are fresh. They can be in the ground one minute and in the pot the next. Once you have tasted fresh vegetables you realize the vast difference between them and the glossy, but days-old ones in the supermarkets. Mass-produced vegetables have been bred to different criteria from those that we grow in the garden. Greengrocers and supermarkets want fruit that will arrive at the shops looking fresh and undamaged, and so the produce has tough skins, which also give them a long shelf life. Fruit and vegetables from the garden do not have to travel.

Farmers want to harvest a crop all at once, so it is important that all the peas, for example, are ready for picking on the same day. Gardeners, on the other hand, want the reverse – they want as long a season as possible. Supermarkets want all the vegetables they stock to be the same size and to look the same, but gardeners, provided they are not interested in exhibiting, are not so fussy.

At the bottom of the list of qualities that are demanded by shops and supermarkets, and frequently not on the list at all, is taste. Customers go back to buy carrots every week without any thought to what the last batch tasted like. Gardeners, however, have a wide choice of carrot seeds, many selected for flavour, and they can choose the variety with the taste they like best.

Another advantage, allied to taste, is that gardeners know what has been put on the food. Today, gardeners choose to use few chemical sprays and powders, but crops bought from supermarkets have been doused in an ever-increasing number of compounds to make sure that, among other things, they come to the shops in a totally unblemished state. Gardeners can know that their food is completely untainted by chemicals.

Garden vegetables are the ultimate in convenience food. Admittedly, you have to wash them, but they sit there just waiting to be harvested when you want them. You may need only one stalk of celery, so why go and buy a whole bunch, when you can quickly cut one stalk from the garden? This is much more economical and saves on time spent shopping. Excess produce can be frozen or stored, and used when you need it.

Kitchen gardens can be decorative, too. Even a simple garden with everything grown in rows or blocks is likely to be attractive, but when they are planted as part of a potager, vegetables can be arranged in even more decorative ways.

Lastly, as well as having healthy food, the gardener gets plenty of exercise and fresh air. There is also a sense of closeness to nature. A cliché perhaps, but there is still something fundamental about getting your hands dirty and listening to the birds as you work.

That is the end of the philosophy of the kitchen garden. From this point the book becomes a practical one. It concentrates on describing the techniques required to produce an attractive and productive kitchen garden. With this book as a guide you will soon not only be growing your own produce but acquiring a whole set of skills, many of them traditional ones, handed down over the centuries, and others that are the result of modern experience.

ABOVE **Here, pink-flowered chives, red lettuce and purple cabbage as well as fennel and parsley create an informal vegetable garden.**

designing
and planning

For most vegetable growers, the ultimate goal is their produce: they want to grow the best possible vegetables. In order to achieve this, the gardener needs to plan his or her crops very carefully, especially if lack of time and the size of garden are possible limitations. There is little point in taking on a large kitchen garden if you cannot maintain it and, similarly, it is inadvisable to expect large harvests from a small plot of ground.

However, with planning and a careful use of space and time, a surprising amount can be grown. Some parts of the planning stage are largely aesthetic, but others will influence the quantity and quality of your crops. Techniques such as crop rotation, successional cropping and intercropping are particularly important in this context.

One of the first decisions to be made is whether to grow the vegetables in rows or in blocks. There are advantages and disadvantages to both systems, and in the end it is really a question of personal choice.

The consideration of all these factors will eventually become second nature to you. The experienced gardener does not have to think twice about them, but if you are approaching kitchen gardening for the first time, it is important to think about them carefully.

The Vegetable Plot

In the working vegetable garden, the overall visual design may not be important. Vegetables are, of course, decorative in their own right, and even the most regimented plot, where everything is grown in rows, usually has some visual appeal. With this type of garden, however, the design is subordinate to convenience and output, with rectangular blocks composed of rows or blocks of crops.

ABOVE **Lack of space is not a problem if you want to grow your own vegetables. Even this small border functions as a working vegetable garden.**

Permanent structures

The first consideration is the position of more permanent items, such as greenhouses, cold frames, sheds and compost bins. The greenhouse needs plenty of light and should be away from cold winds. It should also be near the house because it often needs attention in the winter and at night. This also applies to cold frames. The shed and the compost bins can be more or less anywhere, although not too far away. If the compost bin is a long way away, you may be tempted to leave rotting vegetation lying around rather than clearing up.

All these structures need access paths, which again will dictate their position. A compost bin on the far side of a bed may fill a space, but it will be of little use if you have to walk over the bed to get to it. Putting in a path to it, however, will take up valuable growing space.

Bed design

The positioning of the beds should have prime consideration. Practice varies considerably on the shape and method employed. Most gardeners prefer to have large rectangular plots, 3.6m/12ft wide and as long as the garden allows. Typically, there are two such plots, one each side of a central path. Within these plots rows of vegetables are set out across the beds, with temporary narrow paths between each row.

Recent years have seen the reintroduction of a different method, which had fallen out of favour. This is the use of deep beds, only 1.2m/4ft wide. Such beds, can, in fact, be easily superimposed on the old system by dividing up the long plot into any number of 1.2 x 3.6m/4 x 12ft beds. The significance of the 1.2m/4ft width is that the whole bed can be reached from either side. These smaller beds have permanent paths on each side, which can be paved or left as bare earth.

Permanent planting

Most planting in the kitchen garden is done on an annual basis and changes every year, but there are some plants that stay in the same position for several, if not many, years. Vegetables such as rhubarb, globe artichokes and asparagus need a permanent base. Most fruit is permanent or is moved only every few years. Tree fruit, in particular, must be considered as a long-term addition to the garden.

These types of plants are usually kept together, partly for convenience and partly because they can all be protected against birds by being included in one fruit cage.

Paths

Paths in a productive kitchen garden tend to be for access purposes and not seen as part of a decorative pattern.

RIGHT **This large traditional vegetable garden contains a great variety of foliage, which can be highly decorative.**

A Walled Vegetable Garden

A vegetable garden is basically a utilitarian space for growing vegetables, but it frequently becomes much more than that. Vegetables are decorative in their own right and a well-planned vegetable plot can usually become a very attractive part of the garden.

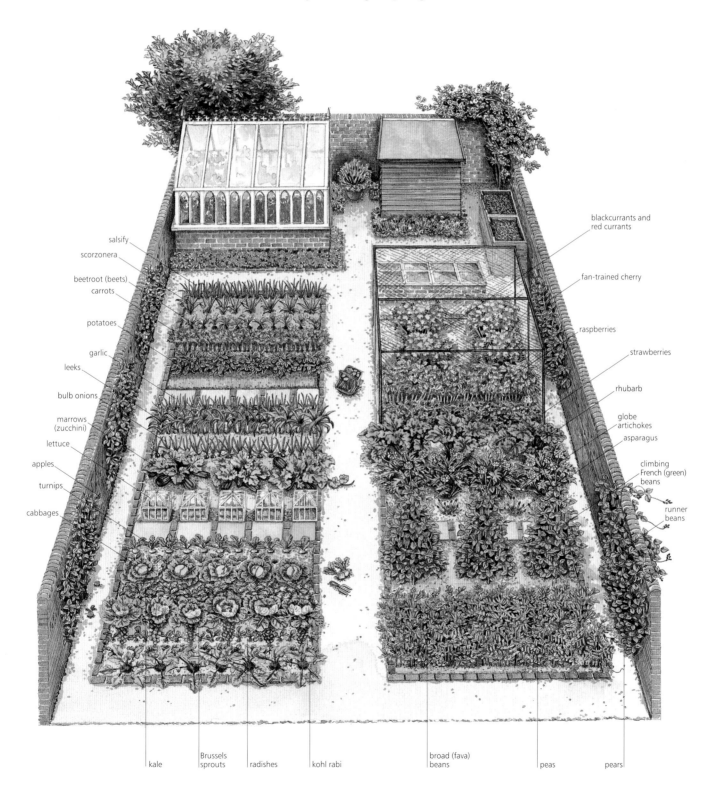

salsify

scorzonera

beetroot (beets)

carrots

potatoes

garlic

leeks

bulb onions

marrows (zucchini)

lettuce

apples

turnips

cabbages

kale

Brussels sprouts

radishes

kohl rabi

broad (fava) beans

peas

pears

blackcurrants and red currants

fan-trained cherry

raspberries

strawberries

rhubarb

globe artichokes

asparagus

climbing French (green) beans

runner beans

Decorative Fruit and Vegetables

One tends to think of vegetables and fruit as being grown either in special gardens or in beds within gardens that are devoted solely to them. There is, however, no reason why they should not be mixed with plants that are grown for decorative purposes. Most gardens have flowering and foliage plants, so why not mix a few vegetables in with them?

ABOVE **Many vegetables are decorative in their own right. Both the flowers and foliage of these climbing beans are purple.**

Decorative vegetables

Some vegetables seem to have been created for inclusion in decorative schemes. Ruby chard, also known as red-stemmed Swiss chard or rhubarb chard, is a perfect example. Although it is good to eat, its vivid red stems and deep purple foliage make it an ideal border plant, particularly in a position where a touch of bright colour is required. Beetroot (beets), while perhaps not quite as colourful, can be used in the same way.

Colour is not all. The foliage of carrots may not be particularly unusual in colour, but it has a wonderful filigree shape and soft texture. These qualities can be used to soften or link two neighbouring colours, or to break up an area of rather solid foliage.

Climbing plants, such as beans, peas, marrows (zucchini) and squashes, can be used to cover arbours and pergolas. Colourful squashes and marrows hanging down in a walkway can be an attractive, if unexpected, sight.

Decorative fruit

Fruit is even more adaptable than vegetables. Apple or plum trees create a dappled shade that is perfect for sitting under or for creating beds in which to grow shade-loving plants. They can be grown against walls as cordons, espaliers or fans, where they create beautiful two-dimensional patterns that can be even more attractive than conventional climbers. In addition to the shape, there are the blossom and the fruit to enjoy, and the leaves of some varieties of pears have wonderful autumn colours.

Walls are not the only way to display trained fruit trees. They can be used to decorate arbours, pergolas and arches. Grapes can also be used in this type of position, rather than training them in a regimented way against wirework in a fruit garden.

Some bush fruit, red currants and gooseberries in particular, can be grown as tree-form standards – that is, they have a thin, unbranched trunk with the "bush" sitting on top. These can look extremely attractive in borders and beds, especially

LEFT **Many vegetables, such as these purple-leaved Brussels sprouts, have dramatic leaves that make a vegetable plot look very striking.**

An Ornamental Fruit Garden

*Fruit gardens should be laid out in the most productive way possible, ensuring
that each plant has sufficient space to grow and develop as well as plenty of air and
light. However, this does not prevent a fruit garden from being designed in an
attractive way that makes the most of the natural beauty of the fruit trees and bushes.*

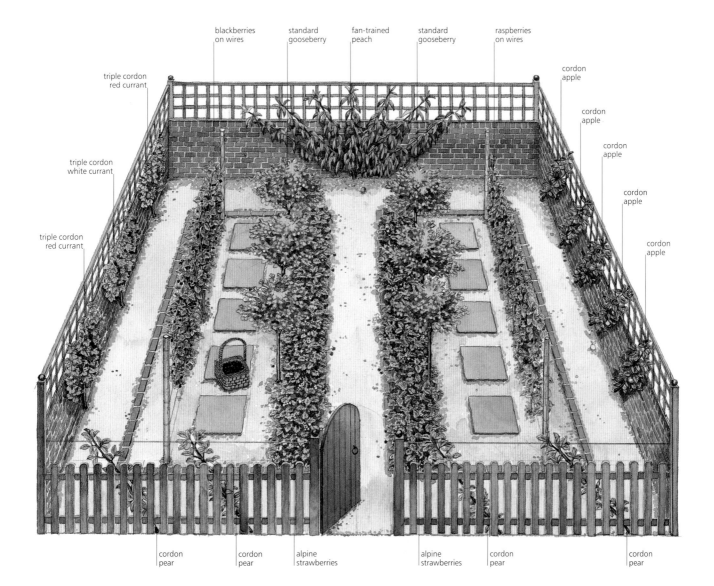

blackberries
on wires

standard
gooseberry

fan-trained
peach

standard
gooseberry

raspberries
on wires

cordon
apple

triple cordon
red currant

cordon
apple

cordon
apple

cordon
apple

triple cordon
white currant

cordon
apple

triple cordon
red currant

cordon
apple

cordon
pear

cordon
pear

alpine
strawberries

alpine
strawberries

cordon
pear

cordon
pear

if they are the centrepiece. Naturally, they
look best when they are in full fruit.

Even strawberries can be used in a decorative manner. Alpine strawberries make
good edging plants for borders. A single line
between the border and a path, for example,
can be extremely effective, especially as they
have a long flowering season. They work
really well around the edge of herb gardens
but can be used in any type of border.

Decorative herbs

Although herbs can be kept together in a
separate garden, they do lend themselves
particularly well to being spread around the
garden in the decorative borders. Shrubby
plants, such as rosemary, sage and thyme,
have an obvious decorative function, but so
do many of the herbaceous varieties. The
thin, grass-like leaves of chives, for example,
contrast well with the bolder shapes of

hostas, and they are also particularly good
for edging paths. The frothy leaves of parsley
can be used in much the same way.

Many herbs can be grown in decorative
borders for their flowers rather than their
leaves. The leaves of bergamot (*Monarda*),
for example, are used as a herb, but the
flowers, which are a bright bold red, are
exceptionally decorative, making this a
superb border plant.

Herb Gardens

Herb gardens tend to fulfil two functions. The first, and obvious one, is to provide herbs. The second arises from the fact that herbs can be highly decorative, making an attractive garden on their own.

Herbs as herbs

Although we grow almost as many herbs as our ancestors, they are primarily included in our gardens for romantic reasons. The number of herbs that most gardeners use in the kitchen is relatively small. But small as this number is, those we do use regularly are important. When you are designing a herb garden, make certain that these herbs are readily accessible from the path, and put those that are never or rarely used in the more inaccessible parts of the border.

The most frequently used herbs should be placed as near to the kitchen door as possible so that the cook can grab a handful when necessary. This means that either the herb garden should be located here or the important herbs should be mixed in with other plants in a decorative border. Another solution is to grow these particular herbs in a container or containers, which can then be placed near the kitchen door for easy access.

Herbs for atmosphere

Although many people regularly use a large number of herbs, most of the gardeners who maintain herb gardens do so because of their romantic associations. And there is no doubt that herbs are romantic. This is partly their history and partly the atmosphere they create in the garden. Herbs tend to be gentle plants, and only occasionally do we come across brash ones. The colours are muted and soft, the atmosphere they create is hazy. On sunny days the garden is perfumed by their scents and is drowsy with the sound of

ABOVE **Coriander (cilantro) is a popular herb with a pungent taste. Its delicate flowers and leaves are also decorative.**

bees. This is the perfect garden in which to sit and relax, so you should remember to include a seat in your design.

Herbs by design

The layout of a herb garden depends largely on the space available, of course, but also on the time you can spend in it. Remember that a large one will take a lot of looking after.

It is possible to create quite small herb gardens, and the herb wheel is one of the most popular plans. An old cartwheel is laid out on prepared ground and the spaces between the spokes are filled with different herbs. When real wheels are not available, the same design can be created from

Important culinary herbs	
Basil	Marjoram
Bay	Mint
Chives	Parsley
Dill	Rosemary
French tarragon	Sage
Lovage	Thyme

LEFT **Box hedges associate well with herb gardens. They add order to what, at times, can be an untidy collection of herbs.**

A Formal Herb Garden

Herb gardens need to be carefully planned if they are to be attractive. Primarily a herb garden is a place for growing herbs for the kitchen, but it should also be a peaceful haven where the scents and colours of the plants can be enjoyed. However, it is worth remembering that a well maintained herb garden needs more attention than a vegetable plot.

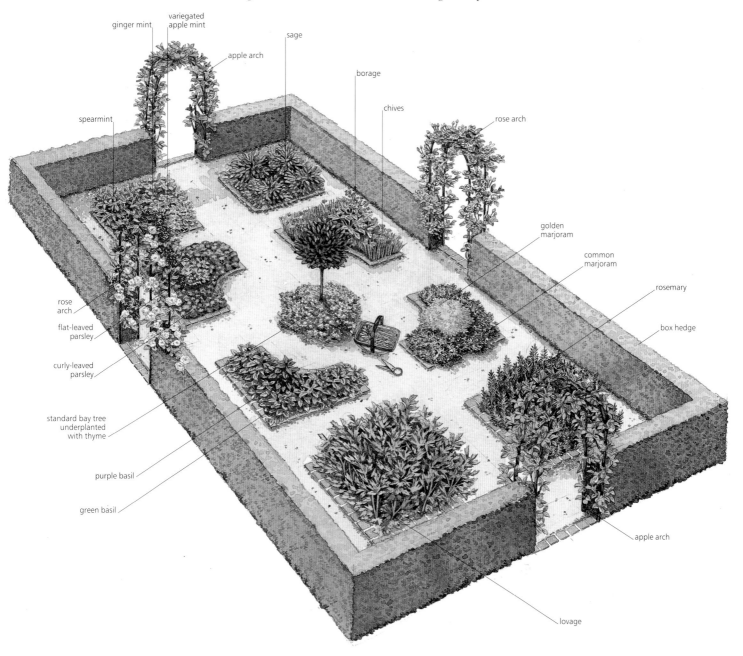

ginger mint
variegated apple mint
apple arch
sage
borage
chives
rose arch
spearmint
golden marjoram
common marjoram
rosemary
box hedge
rose arch
flat-leaved parsley
curly-leaved parsley
standard bay tree underplanted with thyme
purple basil
green basil
apple arch
lovage

bricks. Remember not to use herbs that are too rampant – a sage bush, for example, will soon become big enough to cover the whole area of the wheel. If you want to use the more vigorous plants in a small area, regularly dig them out and replace them.

If you are working on a larger scale, almost any of the patterns mentioned as suitable for potagers can be used. It is worth mentioning that the only time of year when the internal divisions of the garden will be clearly seen is in the winter when the vegetation has died

back. During the growing seasons, the lush growth will be such that the outlines of the beds are not easily seen. If you want to see the demarcations, edge the beds with low box hedges, which will also give good definition to the overall design.

Crop Rotation

Crop rotation has been practised by farmers and gardeners for generations as a simple and effective precaution against pests and diseases. The basic idea is that if you grow the same type of plant on the same patch of ground every year, the soil will harbour pests and diseases from one season to the next. If you move the crop to another piece of ground, the pests and diseases will lose their host and will die out.

ABOVE **In a four-year rotation, courgettes (zucchini) would be grown in plot three. Alternatively, they can be grown on a compost heap.**

The practical side of this philosophy is the division of the vegetable garden into four or five areas. The different types of crops – brassicas, beans and so on – are moved from one plot to another so that they return to the same piece of ground only every fourth year.

For four-year crop rotation, the crops are divided into four groups – the fifth bed is used for the permanent plants, which obviously do not move. Look at the list of vegetables that you wish to grow for the coming year and divide them into their various groups. Allocate planting areas to each. Do the same for the following year, but move all the crops to another plot. If space is limited, a three-year rotation is better than nothing.

BELOW **Globe artichokes stay in the ground for several years, so they are grown in a permanent plot and do not form part of the rotation plan.**

Four-Year Crop Rotation

Plot 1
Peas
Broad (fava) beans
French (green) beans
Runner beans

Plot 2
Cabbages
Brussels sprouts
Calabrese (Italian sprouting broccoli)
Broccoli
Kale
Radishes
Swedes (rutabaga or yellow turnips)
Turnips
Kohl rabi

Plot 3
Bulb onions
Spring onions (scallions)
Shallots
Leeks
Garlic
Sweet corn (corn)
Marrows (zucchini), squashes and pumpkins
Lettuce

Plot 4
Potatoes
Parsnips
Beetroot (beets)
Carrots
Salsify
Scorzonera
Celery
Celeriac (celery root)
Tomatoes

Plot 5 (permanent)
Rhubarb
Asparagus
Perennial herbs
Globe artichokes
Jerusalem artichokes
Seakale

Four-Year Crop Rotation

*In many gardens, the differentiation between the plots is hardly discernible,
but it makes life easier to split the garden into individual plots.*

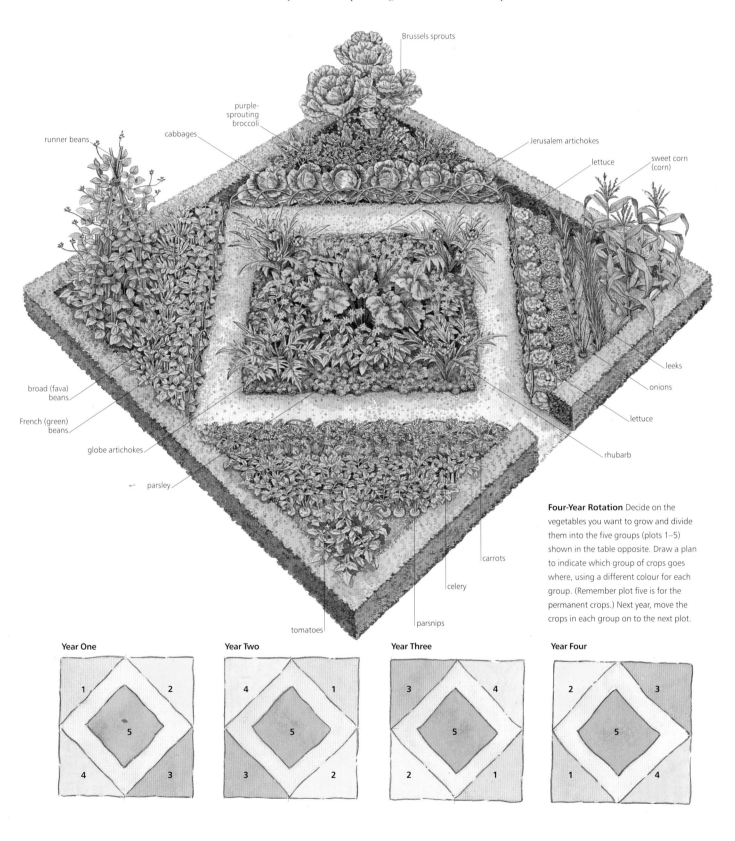

Brussels sprouts

purple-
sprouting
broccoli

cabbages

runner beans

Jerusalem artichokes

lettuce

sweet corn
(corn)

leeks

onions

lettuce

broad (fava)
beans

French (green)
beans

rhubarb

globe artichokes

parsley

carrots

celery

parsnips

tomatoes

Four-Year Rotation Decide on the
vegetables you want to grow and divide
them into the five groups (plots 1–5)
shown in the table opposite. Draw a plan
to indicate which group of crops goes
where, using a different colour for each
group. (Remember plot five is for the
permanent crops.) Next year, move the
crops in each group on to the next plot.

Year One

1 2
5
4 3

Year Two

4 1
5
3 2

Year Three

3 4
5
2 1

Year Four

2 3
5
1 4

Three-Year Crop Rotation

This is a more conventional method of dividing up the garden into separate plots, keeping each group of plants together for rotating.

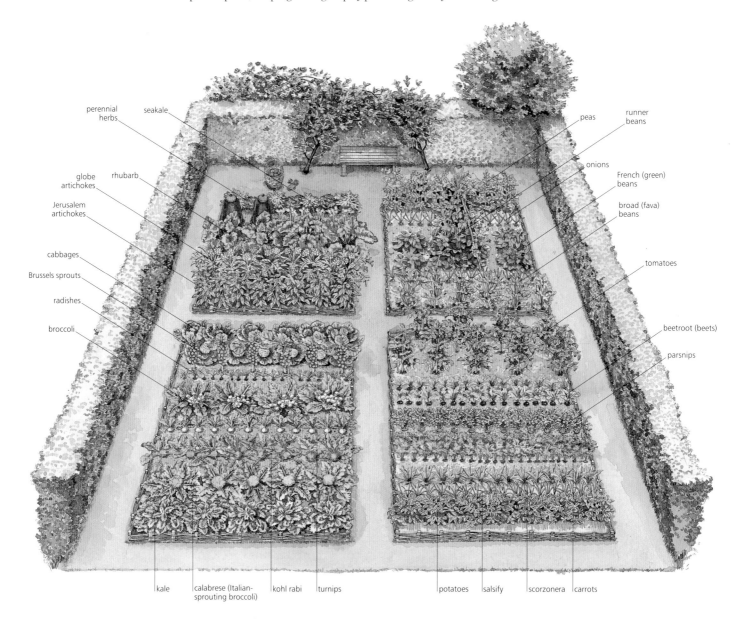

perennial herbs

seakale

globe artichokes

rhubarb

Jerusalem artichokes

cabbages

Brussels sprouts

radishes

broccoli

peas

runner beans

onions

French (green) beans

broad (fava) beans

tomatoes

beetroot (beets)

parsnips

kale

calabrese (Italian-sprouting broccoli)

kohl rabi

turnips

potatoes

salsify

scorzonera

carrots

Three-Year Rotation

Decide on the vegetables you want to grow and divide into the four groups (plots 1–4) shown in the table opposite. Draw a plan to indicate which group of crops goes where, using a different colour for each group. (Remember plot four is for permanent crops.) Move the crops in each group to the next plot the following year.

Year One

4	1
3	2

Year Two

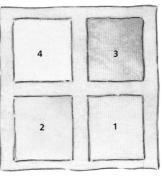

4	3
2	1

Year Three

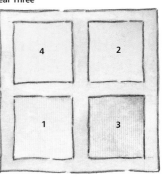

4	2
1	3

Three-Year Crop Rotation

Plot 1
Peas
Broad (fava) beans
French (green) beans
Runner beans
Bulb onions
Leeks
Sweet corn (corn)
Marrows (zucchini), squashes and pumpkins
Lettuce

Plot 2
Potatoes
Parsnips
Beetroot (beets)
Carrots
Salsify
Scorzonera
Tomatoes

Plot 3
Cabbages
Brussels sprouts
Calabrese (Italian sprouting broccoli)
Broccoli
Kale
Swede (rutabaga or yellow turnips)
Turnips
Kohl rabi
Radishes

Plot 4 (permanent)
Rhubarb
Asparagus
Perennial herbs
Globe artichokes
Jerusalem artichokes
Seakale

ABOVE **In a three-year crop rotation, tomatoes are grown in plot two, along with root crops such as parsnips and carrots.**

ABOVE **Rhubarb is planted in the permanent bed when crops are rotated, and can stay in the same position for up to 25 years.**

As well as having advantages in terms of pests and diseases, there are other reasons for moving crops around. Some crops will tolerate newly manured ground while others cannot. Thus, one plot can be heavily manured when it is dug in the autumn during the first year and cabbages and related plants can be planted in it in spring. In the following year the plot is simply dug, and the root crops, which do not like the soil too rich, are planted there.

Strict crop rotation is not the easiest of things to maintain. Many gardeners start off with good intentions and manage it for a few years, but gradually things begin to slip. Some brassicas that have been left in

the ground over winter may block the space that is required for some other plants, or perhaps a few plants have been slipped in to fill a gap. Leaving plants in the ground until the following year so that you can collect your own seeds also plays havoc with rotation if you have only a small amount of space. If you find this happening, there is no need to worry.

In a small kitchen garden, crop rotation, although it is admirable in theory, is not that important in practice. One of the main difficulties is the amount of space required to put strict rotation into effect. In agricultural situations the crops are fields apart; even in a large garden, the distances involved can be

quite large. In a small garden, however, it is often impossible to get the plots far enough apart for the pests or diseases not to be able to find their host plant. The other problem is that, in practice, four years is not always long enough to kill off all the diseases anyway.

This does not mean that crop rotation is unimportant, however, because it still has some effect. Yet it does mean that you should not lose any sleep if you are not able to follow the sequence to the exact letter. Most gardeners do not grow the same crop on the same ground for two years running in any case – with the exception of plants such as runner beans – but they do not follow strict crop rotation.

Rows

Vegetables have traditionally been grown in rows. Although some gardeners challenge the claims made for this method, suggesting that blocks and deep beds are better, rows are probably still the most widely used system.

The basic idea is simple: the vegetables are grown in a single line, with some crops, such as beans and peas, being grown in a double line. The lines or rows are separated by a distance somewhat wider than the breadth of the plants, so that there is bare earth between the rows. This bare earth acts as a path, allowing access for maintenance, such as weeding and watering, as well as for harvesting.

Growing vegetables in rows is an attractive way of producing them. The varying heights, shapes, textures and colours all show up well, with the rows looking like decorative ribbons stretched across the garden. Their appearance is not, however, the principal reason for growing vegetables in this way. There are practical considerations, too.

Access is one of the important benefits provided by individual rows. The paths between the rows allow the gardener to move freely among the plants without having to stretch. Each plant can be examined for condition as well as for pests and diseases. Pests have less chance of being overlooked if the plant can be clearly seen from at least two sides, and individual plants can be tended to if necessary. The bases of the plants can be easily seen for inspection, weeding and watering.

Another advantage is that there is plenty of air circulating among the plants, which helps considerably to reduce mildew-type diseases. The plants generally have plenty of space in which to develop, and the leaves are able to open out to receive the maximum amount of light. Finally, rows are easy to cover with the majority of cloches available.

Needless to say there are also disadvantages. The use of so many "paths" means that a lot of space is unproductive when you look at the plot as a whole, an important factor in a small garden, where space is limited. Another disadvantage is that the paths allow

light to reach the soil, so increasing the number of weeds that germinate, although this is offset to some extent by the ease with which it is possible to hoe. With constant use, the paths become compacted, which does not help the soil structure. Although the whole bed will be dug each year, because it is so large it is necessary to walk over it

LEFT **Traditional rows of vegetables, filling all the available space, can be very decorative.**

while the ground is being prepared, again adding a certain degree of compaction. Constant hoeing will help overcome this by breaking up the soil and keeping it aerated. However, in dry weather, hoeing should be avoided as it encourages water loss. An alternative is to lay planks of wood between the rows. This not only helps to prevent soil compaction but also acts as a mulch which will help retain the moisture in the soil as well as keep weeds down.

ABOVE **The decorative quality of vegetables can be clearly seen in these rows. All the leaves are green and yet the variety of greens and the shapes of the leaves form a very attractive picture over a long season.**

LEFT **It is important to leave plenty of space for young plants to fill out. Rows with plenty of space between them also allow for access and easy weeding.**

Blocks and Deep Beds

Growing vegetables in blocks as opposed to rows is an old method that more or less dropped out of use in many countries but that has been reintroduced in recent years. The basic idea is to grow the plants in a square or rectangle, say five plants wide by five plants deep, rather than in a single row.

The vegetable plot is divided into smaller plots, each about 1.2m/4ft across and spanning the width of the main plot. These smaller beds are permanent, unlike rows, and between each is a path, either trodden earth or more substantial paving slabs or bricks. The width of the smaller beds is determined by the gardener's reach – 1.2m/4ft should allow access of about 60cm/24in from each side so that the entire bed can be reached without compacting the soil. Keeping off the beds means that the soil structure is always kept in top condition.

Some gardeners simply dig the soil in the existing plot, adding organic material to it as they go. Others prefer to create a deep bed system, either by digging deeper, using a double digging method, or by raising the height of the bed with boards or a low wall and then adding a mixture of good loam and organic material. The bed is worked from the path so that the soil is never compacted.

The advantage of a rich soil in good condition is that it will support more plants, and so most gardeners plant much more closely than in the conventional rows. This means that productivity is improved considerably, and many more plants can be raised from the same area of ground. As well as being productive, close planting also means that weed seeds have little chance of germinating.

A solid block of plants, however, makes it more difficult to get at any weeds, as well as making it harder to see if there are any pests and diseases lurking below the leaves. Because the plants are close together, there is likely to be less air circulating than around vegetables grown in rows, and this increases the possibility of diseases that like damp conditions with stagnant air. It is also not as

RIGHT **Each of these blocks of vegetables and herbs is about 1.2m/4ft wide, which allows access from the paths running across the plot.**

easy to water the base of individual plants. Watering can, in fact, become erratic, with some areas ending up drier than others as water runs off the leaves. Another disadvantage is that it is not as easy to cover the vegetables with cloches, and although it is, of course, possible to construct a cover, this will not be as mobile as individual cloches.

You can take advantage of both methods by using deep beds, with their rich soil conditions, and planting short rows across the beds instead of blocks. This method works well for those gardeners who feel that digging destroys the structure of the soil. They dig the soil initially, adding plenty of organic material, but thereafter only top-dress the surface with more organic material, perhaps hoeing it in or allowing the worms to move it below the surface. Although this benefits the soil, most gardeners prefer the more traditional method of digging at least once a year because this has other advantages.

LEFT **Boards create a greater depth of fertile soil, so vegetables can be planted much closer together.**

Intercropping

There can be few gardeners who have enough space to grow everything they wish, and this is particularly true of those with small gardens. One way partly to overcome the problem is to make sure that every available piece of land is in use and to avoid letting ground lie idle.

There are two main ways to ensure that the land is used efficiently. The first is to plant quick-growing crops among slower ones so that the former have been harvested before the latter have grown sufficiently to fill the space. Brussels sprouts, for example, are planted at anything up to 75cm/30in apart, depending on the size of the variety. For several weeks after they have been planted there is a lot of empty space around each plant. This can be filled with a crop such as lettuce or radishes that takes only a short while to come to maturity.

Some plants, however, cannot be planted out in the early part of the season, and rather than leave the ground empty, it can be filled with a temporary crop. For example, a bed of lettuces can be planted and the first ones to be harvested can be replaced by young sweet corn (corn), the rest of the lettuces being harvested as the corn develops.

A similar idea can be used with station-sown seeds. For example, parsnip seeds can be sown in groups of three at, say, 23cm/9in intervals. In between each group a few radishes can be sown. This method has advantages in that not only will the quick-growing radishes make use of the ground before the parsnips need it, but, because parsnips are slow to germinate, the radishes will actually mark the row, making it easier to hoe off any weeds without disturbing the parsnips, which are still below ground.

Another aspect of intercropping is purely decorative. A simple example is to intercrop red-leaved lettuces with green ones.

To create these effects, it is best to raise the plants in trays or modules and plant them out in a pattern when they are large enough.

When you are intercropping for visual effects, take care in the choice of neighbours. There is little point in planting decorative lettuces next to potatoes, which will eventually flop over and smother them. However, from the productive point of view it is a good idea to plant lettuces between rows of potatoes before the latter have emerged or have reached any height, because the lettuces will be cropped before the ground is smothered by the potato leaves.

ABOVE **Here, a short row of radishes is being sown between individual cabbages. They will crop long before the cabbages have grown large enough to cover them.**

ABOVE **As an alternative to sowing, individual lettuces can be planted between slow-growing plants such as cabbages.**

BELOW **Intercropping carrots with lettuces – here a tinted variety known as 'Nelson' – makes for a very decorative effect.**

Successional Crops

Closely related to the question of intercropping is that of successional sowing and planting. The idea behind this is to phase the crops so that your plot provides a continuous stream of produce and not a series of sudden gluts. In other words, this is another method of ensuring that you get the most out of your ground.

Many gardeners have a tendency to sow a complete row right across their plot, whether they need that amount of produce or not, simply because a whole row looks better than a short one. This can be wasteful, because two-thirds of the row may bolt before you have consumed it and then you are left with nothing. It is far better to sow a third of a row of, say, spinach, wait two or three weeks and then sow another third and finally the last section two or three weeks later still. This means that the crops will reach maturity at two- to three-week intervals, spreading out so that you have spinach for two months or more rather than for the two to three weeks that would have been the case if you had sown the whole row at once.

Another way of securing a succession of crops is to choose varieties that mature at different times. Peas, for example, are classified into first earlies and maincrop types, and within these groups some varieties produce peas sooner than others. Choosing several different varieties rather than just one will provide a much longer harvesting season.

The same principle is true of fruit. Choosing different varieties of raspberries, for example, will enable you to harvest fruit from early summer right through to late autumn. This also applies to strawberries, apples and many other types of fruit.

There may, of course, be times when you do not want to spread the harvesting. For example, if you like to freeze vegetables for winter use it is easier if, for example, all your peas mature at once so that you can quickly freeze them and replant the ground with another crop of something else – late turnips perhaps. Vegetables that all crop at once are usually marked in the seed catalogues as being suitable for freezing.

If you are creating a vegetable garden as a decorative feature as well as a productive one, successional sowing and planting becomes doubly important. Any crop removed, whether it is a single lettuce or a row or a wigwam (tepee) of peas will leave a gap and the sooner it is filled the better the garden will look.

Both from the productive and the visual point of view it is always worthwhile having a few plants coming along in pots ready to plant out. Lettuce, Swiss chard and parsley, for example, can be sown at two-week intervals in modules to provide a good supply of plants to fill the gaps.

Another aspect of successional cropping is replacing one crop with another as soon as it is finished. Thus, replant the ground occupied by broad (fava) beans with a late crop of leeks as the beans are finished or plant out spring cabbage in the space that becomes available when the onions are harvested. Keep the ground producing for you even if you only sow green manure, which is dug back into the soil later in the year.

RIGHT **Some crops are better planted at intervals so that they do not all mature at the same time. To facilitate this, it is often easier to fill long rows with several different types of vegetables rather than leave gaps to be sown later.**

equipment

Considering the large number of tools and equipment that is now available from the average garden centre, the gardener can actually get by with buying surprisingly few of them, as long as they are chosen carefully and with a view to what is actually needed. Starting a vegetable garden need not be a costly business. You do not, for example, have to invest in a large greenhouse or in cold frames, although a shed will prove useful if you do not want to perform unhygienic gardening tasks in the kitchen. A wheelbarrow is the only mechanical device that most gardeners will require although many may use a rotavator (rototiller) for digging larger plots. There are also many excellent second-hand tools to be had, very often at a fraction of the price of new ones that may be of an inferior quality, so it is worth spending a little time on finding the best tools.

Greenhouses

The ultimate goal of most gardeners is to have a greenhouse, for it extends the possibilities of the garden tremendously. Such a structure can be used for propagation, for growing tender or winter crops and for overwintering plants that cannot be safely left outside. There is a fourth, often unspoken, use and that is to keep the gardener dry and warm in winter.

Most of the horticultural operations that are done in a greenhouse can be achieved perfectly satisfactorily in cold frames. Most gardeners, however, prefer to carry them out in the warmth and comfort of the greenhouse, rather than bending over a cold frame in a cold or wet wind.

Choosing a greenhouse

As with any equipment, the first thing to consider are your reasons for making the purchase. Why do you want a greenhouse? What are you going to do with it? This is an important stage, because answering these questions will help to determine the size.

BELOW **This standard straight-sided greenhouse is made of aluminium, but it has been painted green, rather than being left silver, so that it blends in better with the colours of the garden.**

Cost and the available space will also obviously influence the size, but if possible, make use the prime consideration. Most gardeners, slightly tongue in cheek, will tell you to work out the size and then double it. There is some truth in this old saw, and many, if not most, gardeners wish that they had bought a larger greenhouse than the one they did. So buy larger rather than smaller if you possibly can.

Material

These days the choice is mainly between wood and aluminium, although it is still possible to find old iron-frame greenhouses, and some more expensive ones are a combination of materials, such as brick and wood. For most gardeners the choice is simply an aluminium frame, because it is the cheapest style available, but there are other factors to be taken into consideration. For example,

ABOVE **The marigolds planted with a row of tomatoes in this greenhouse will ward off potential pests, a technique known as companion planting.**

wooden greenhouses are far more attractive than aluminium ones. However, although they usually fit more sympathetically into the garden, they are more expensive and the upkeep is more time-consuming. Wooden greenhouses are slightly warmer in winter. It is possible to make your own, working to your own design and dimensions.

Aluminium greenhouses are cheap and easy to maintain. The cheaper ones may, however, be rather flimsy, and in exposed positions the sides may flex and the glass fall out! They normally come in standard sizes, but because they are modular, there is a choice of the number of windows and their position. Some companies will build to your specifications, but this is obviously a more expensive option. It is now possible to buy aluminium greenhouses where the frame is painted, which partially disguises the aluminium.

Glass can now be replaced with plastic. Most gardeners prefer the traditional material, but if there are children around it is often more sensible to go for plastic on safety grounds.

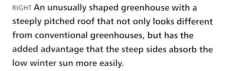

RIGHT **An unusually shaped greenhouse with a steeply pitched roof that not only looks different from conventional greenhouses, but has the added advantage that the steep sides absorb the low winter sun more easily.**

Digging in

The old-fashioned idea of sinking the green-house into the ground is a good one as long as you can overcome any drainage problems. Steps lead down to the door, and on to a central aisle, dug out of the soil. The side benches are laid on the natural soil level and the roof springs from a low wall on the ground. The advantage of this system, apart from the fact that it is relatively cheap, is that the soil acts as a vast storage heater. Gardeners using such a greenhouse find that as long as they provide some form of insulation, no heat is required to overwinter tender plants. Traditionally, a wooden framework would have been used for the roof, but aluminium would do just as well.

Shape

The shape of the greenhouse is a matter of personal preference. Traditional styles have vertical sides, but some new ones have sloping sides, which allow in more light – especially useful during winter when the sun is low or if you have trays of seedlings on the floor.

Octagonal greenhouses are suitable for small sites, and many people find them more decorative than the traditional shapes. Because they are almost round, the "aisle" is just a central standing area, thus saving a lot of wasted space. However, the amount of useful space is still quite small.

Lean-to greenhouses can be built against walls, which not only saves space but also makes use of the warmth that is usually found in the wall, especially house walls. These are obviously much cheaper than a full greenhouse, but the amount of useful space within them is limited because the light does not come from all directions and plants can get drawn. Painting the wall white helps because more light is reflected back onto the plants.

Ventilation

When you buy a greenhouse, make sure that it has as many opening windows as you can afford because the free passage of air through the structure is of the utmost

ABOVE **Insulating the greenhouse is important during the cold winter months, helping to keep heating costs down as well as preventing any violent fluctuations in temperature. Polythene (plastic) bubble insulation is cheap and efficient.**

LEFT **Some plants, such as peppers, grow better in a greenhouse than they do outside in the open air. In a greenhouse, they are assured of a constant temperature and humidity.**

importance. Stagnant air in a greenhouse is a killer, as all kinds of fungal diseases are likely to develop very quickly. Openings can either be covered with conventional windows or with louvres. If you are away during daylight hours in summer, the time when windows need to be opened on hot days, automatic openers can be used. The mechanism opens the windows as soon as a specified pre-set temperature is reached. Having a door at each end helps on larger houses. In winter, windows should be left open as much as possible, and, when it is necessary to close them, use a fan to keep the air circulating.

Heating

There are various methods of heating a greenhouse, but one of the most versatile is with electricity. Although the cost per unit of heat may be greater, the control of its output through the use of thermostats is such that no heat (or money) is wasted, because the appliance comes on only when the temperature drops below a certain point. Thermostatically controlled gas heaters are also now becoming available. Paraffin heaters are cheap, but they need to be regularly filled and maintained and they produce large amounts of water vapour, which encourages disease unless the greenhouse is ventilated.

Heating bills can be reduced by insulating the greenhouse. Double glazing is the ultimate but is expensive. A cheaper alternative is to line the house with sheets of clear polythene (plastic), preferably containing air bubbles. If you have only a few plants that need protecting, it is cheaper to close off one end of the greenhouse with polythene and heat just this area. If the number of plants is small enough, a heated propagator or a cloche over a heated bench may be sufficient.

Shading

Greenhouses need to be as light as possible, especially during the winter, but at the same time bright sunshine should be kept out as this will raise the temperature too much. It is possible to buy shade netting, which can be draped over the outside or clipped to the inside of the glass. This is easy to remove in overcast periods. An opaque wash applied to the glass reduces the effect of

the sun considerably, but it is time-consuming to keep removing it during dull weather, so it is usually left in place from early summer to mid-autumn. There is one form of wash that becomes transparent when it rains, thus letting in more light.

Fittings

The full height of the greenhouse is needed for tomatoes and cucumbers, which can be grown in growing bags on the floor. Benching or staging is a useful addition, at least down one side, and can be made of wood or longer-lasting aluminium.

If the staging has raised sides it can be filled with sand. This is useful for sinking pots in to help keep them warm and moist. Heating cables can also be used to keep the bench warm, and building a polythene (plastic) or glass cabinet or lid on top will turn it into an effective propagating bench.

Polytunnels

Polythene (plastic) tunnels are a cheap alternative to greenhouses. They are ideal for growing winter and early spring vegetables and for housing and propagating plants until they are ready to plant out. They are, however, rather ugly and can get very cold, and the polythene will need replacing every three years or so.

Tools and Equipment

To look in the average garden centre you would imagine that you need a tremendous battery of tools and equipment before you could ever consider gardening, but in fact you can start (and continue) gardening with relatively few tools and no equipment at all.

Tools are personal things, so one gardener may always use a spade for digging, no matter how soft the ground, whereas another would always use a fork as long as the ground was not too heavy. The type of hoe for certain jobs is another subject on which gardeners hold widely different opinions.

Buying tools

It is not necessary to buy a vast armoury of tools when you first start gardening. Most of the jobs can be done with a small basic kit.

When you are buying, always choose the best you can afford. Many of the cheaper tools are made of pressed steel, which soon becomes blunt, will often bend and may even break. Stainless steel is undoubtedly the best, but tools made of this tend to be expensive. Ordinary steel implements can be almost as good, especially if you keep them clean. Avoid tools that are made of aluminium. Trowels and hand forks especially are often made of aluminium, but they wear down and blunt quickly and are not good value for money.

Soil Testers
The chemical composition of the soil can be tested by the gardener by using one of a range of soil testers. The most commonly used checks the acidity/alkalinity of the soil. It is chemical based and involves mixing soil samples with water and checking the colour against a chart. More complicated tests indicate whether there is a shortage of minerals or trace elements. The balance can then be adjusted by adding lime or fertilizers to the soil.

ACIDITY
Alkaline
Neutral
Acid
Very Acid

Second-hand

A good way to acquire a collection of tools is to buy them second-hand. There are advantages to this. One is that they are usually much cheaper than new ones. Frequently, too, they are made of much better steel than cheap, modern ones and still retain a keen edge, even after many years' use. In the past gardening tools were made with a much greater variation in design and size. If you go to buy a modern spade, for example, you will probably find that the sizes in the shop are all the same – designed for the "average" gardener. Old tools come in all shapes and

spade

fork

Labelling and Tying
When working in the garden, it is useful to have a tray of odds and ends, such as string, raffia, plant ties and labels. You never know when you might need them. For example, it is always difficult to remember what has been planted or sown where – it may be weeks before seed you have sown is visible above ground.

raffia

plant ties

string

plant labels

trowel

hand fork

dibber

pruning saw

sizes, and if you find modern tools uncomfortable to use you are more likely to find an old one that is made just for you.

Not all old tools are good by any means, of course, but by keeping an eye out and buying only good quality ones you will end up with tools that will more than see you through your gardening career and at a relatively modest price. Car boot fairs (garage sales) and rural junk shops (second-hand stores) are the places to look out for them. Avoid antique shops where such tools are sold at inflated prices to be hung as decorations on the wall rather than to be used.

Care and maintenance

Look after your tools. If you do this they will not only always be in tip-top working condition but will last a lifetime. Scrape all the mud and any vegetation off the tools as soon as you have used them. Once they are clean, run an oily rag lightly over the metal parts. The thin film of oil will stop the metal from corroding. This not only makes the tools last longer but also makes them easier to use because less effort is needed to use a clean spade than one with a rough surface of rust.

In addition, keep the wooden parts clean, wiping them over with linseed oil if the wood becomes too dry.

Keep all blades sharp. Hang tools up if possible. Standing spades and hoes on the ground, especially if it is concrete, will blunt them over time. Keep them away from children.

Equipment

It is possible to run a vegetable and fruit garden with no mechanical aids at all. However, if you have grass paths, a lawn mower will, obviously, be more than useful – it will be essential. Hedge cutters, too, are useful, although hedges can be cut by hand much more easily than grass paths.

In the vegetable garden itself the only mechanical device that you may require is a rotavator (rototiller), which can be used for digging and breaking up the soil. Unless you have a large garden, however, this is not absolutely necessary, although it does make life easier if you want to break down a heavy soil into a fine tilth.

Keep all your equipment maintained. There is nothing worse than wanting a piece of machinery to use in a hurry only to find that it will not start. After the weather, machinery is the most stressful part of gardening.

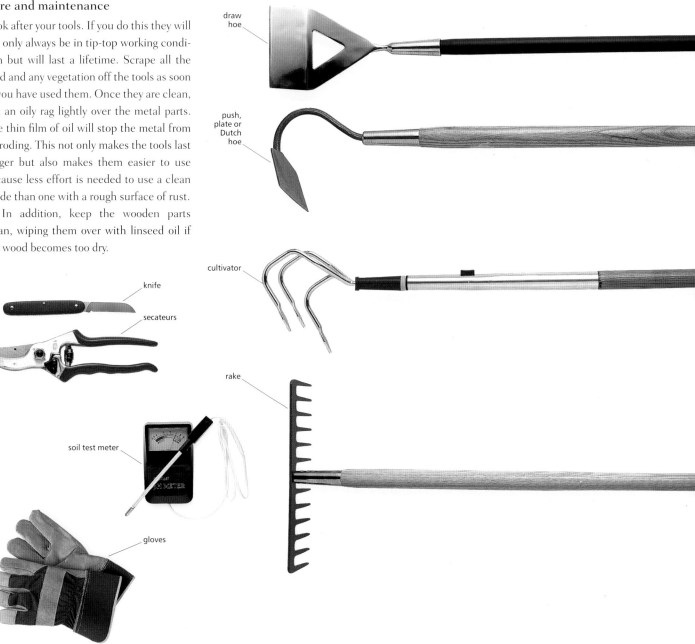

draw hoe

push, plate or Dutch hoe

cultivator

rake

knife

secateurs

soil test meter

gloves

Cold Frames

Cold frames are rather underrated by many gardeners. They are not only useful in their own right but they can also be used for most of the jobs that are undertaken in the greenhouse. They are less expensive than greenhouses, take up less space and are cheaper to keep warm. Their main disadvantage is that the gardener works outside and not inside in the warm and dry as with a greenhouse.

Uses

In the vegetable garden, cold frames are frequently used for producing winter or early crops of such vegetables as carrots. The frame can be in a permanent position in the garden or moved, rather like a large cloche, onto the vegetable bed itself. The vegetables can be grown either directly in the soil or in growing bags. Later in the year, the cold frame can be used for growing cucumbers or melons.

Another basic use is to afford protection and warmth to trays of seeds or seedlings. Once the plants are ready to go out, the lights can be opened over a period of a week or two to harden off the plants before they are planted out.

Materials

As with greenhouses, the cheaper cold frames are made from aluminium. Their advantage is that they are light enough to move around, but they are not good at retaining heat. Wooden ones are better at this, and cold frames with solid walls made from brick, concrete or even old railway sleepers (ties) provide much better protection during the winter.

Aluminium-framed cold frames can be designed to include glass in the sides, which allows in more light. Solid-sided ones are much warmer but light can enter only through the glass above. It is a good idea to paint the inside of the walls white to reflect some of the light.

Lights (lids) that are glazed with glass are generally preferable, but plastic can be used where there is danger of accidents – if children or elderly people are in the garden, for example.

Heating

Most cold frames, as their name suggests, are not heated. However, it is easier and cheaper to provide some warmth than in a greenhouse, and if you want to propagate or overwinter tender plants it may be possible to supply some form of heat. Electric heating cables installed in the sand below the pots and around the walls of the frame is the easiest method. It is also the most efficient if the cables are connected to a thermostat that switches the electricity on only when heat is required.

Hotbeds

A traditional way to heat cold frames is to set them on a pile of farmyard manure, usually horse dung. As the dung breaks down it releases more than enough heat to keep the frames warm. Soil can be laid on top of the manure and a wide range of vegetables grown in it during the winter. The manure should be fresh, and once it has rotted down and no longer generates heat, it can be spread on the garden and dug in.

Insulation

It is easy to insulate cold frames because they are small. The simplest way is to throw an old carpet over the frame on cold nights.

LEFT **When the seedlings are fully acclimatized and ready to be planted out, the lights (lids) can be left off altogether.**

This may be sufficient to hold in the residual heat, so no extra heating is required to keep the frame above freezing. More efficient methods would be to cover the frames with bubble polythene (plastic) or even to line the inside of the lights with it.

Ventilation

When it is not necessary to keep the frames tightly shut to avoid heat loss, it is sensible to open them slightly, even if it is just a crack, to let air circulate among the plants. This helps prevent various fungal diseases, especially botrytis, which cause seedlings to die through rotting.

RIGHT **A cold frame with a partially opened light (lid) so that the greenhouse-grown seedlings gradually become acclimatized to the outside conditions.**

BELOW **A brick cold frame with a soil bed for growing winter and early spring vegetables.**

Cloches

Cloches are portable forms of protection, rather like miniature cold frames. They are mainly employed during the winter and early spring, but they can be used at any time of year to bring on a crop or to protect it.

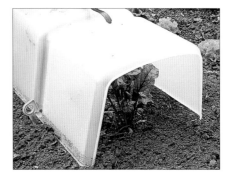

ABOVE **A rigid plastic cloche is easy to use. The sections butt up against each other and can be pegged into the soil. Endpieces are also available.**

Uses

There are frequently times when you want to cosset a few plants. They may need protection from the cold or it may be that they are not particularly worried by the cold but need a little warmth to make them grow faster. One row of strawberries, for example, can be covered with cloches to make them fruit one or even two weeks earlier than they would if uncovered. During the winter, broad (fava) beans will come on better if they are protected not only from the cold but also the extremes of rain and wind. Cloches can also be used to protect plants from predators.

In wet and cold areas cloches can be used to cover the ground so that it both dries out and warms up ready for sowing. This will often enable the gardener to sow several weeks earlier than the weather would otherwise allow in the unprotected garden.

In autumn, cloches can be used to cover ripening or harvested vegetables. For example, cordon tomatoes can be lowered to the ground onto straw and allowed to ripen under cloches, while onions that have been harvested in a wet summer can be placed under cloches to "harden off" before storing.

Materials

Some of the earliest cloches were glass bell jars – like upside-down glass vases – which were placed over individual plants. Other traditional cloches were made from sheets of glass, and the earliest types were held in iron frameworks, and resembled miniature greenhouses. Later, cloches became simpler, and the glass was held together by metal or, more recently, plastic or rubber clips. These were known as barn or tent cloches because of their shapes, and could cover a single plant or a whole row when arranged in a line.

Glass is still used, but most cloches are made of polythene (sheet vinyl or plastic) or rigid plastic. There are two main types. One is made up of individual units, which link up in some way, and the other is like a miniature polytunnel, with a single sheet of polythene stretched along the length of the row.

All cloches will do the job they are designed to do. Glass should last the longest, unless you are careless. Although plastics and polythene (sheet vinyl) have a more limited lifespan, they are generally cheaper to replace and are usually lighter and easier to store.

Making your own

Bought cloches may not fit the length or width of the rows in your garden, especially if you are growing in deep beds or blocks. It is relatively simple to make your own. For smaller rows, several hoops of galvanized wire are pushed into the earth at intervals of 60cm/24in and a sheet of polythene (plastic) is laid over them. Place more wire hoops over the first, so that the polythene is trapped between them and held securely. For real security the sides and the two ends of the polythene can be buried in the earth.

For larger beds hoops can be made from lengths of plastic water pipe. Place a stick or iron stake in the ground on each side of the block or row and place the end of the pipe over the stake, forming a hoop. Proceed as before, using more hoops to hold the polythene (plastic) in place, or use strings stretched over the polythene next to the hoops and attached to wire hooks sunk into the ground.

LEFT **Glass bell jars are simple cloches for covering one plant. They are expensive, but plastic sweet jars make a good, if not as attractive, alternative.**

RIGHT **Old-fashioned cloches are particularly good for decorative vegetable gardens. However, they are also very expensive.**

soil

The soil in your garden is your most valuable asset, and it should be cared for accordingly. Some gardeners are lucky and inherit soil in good condition, others find that their soil was once good but is now a little tired and in need of attention. Unlucky gardeners start with virgin soil, often a heavy clay and filled with builder's rubble. Even good soil needs care, while the other two types of soil, especially the heavy soil, need plenty of attention. However, given time and energy even a heavy soil will become fertile and workable, and produce good vegetables.

The main tool in the gardener's armoury is organic material: farmyard manure, garden compost and many other well-rotted forms of humus. It is never possible to have too much of this if you want good soil. Gravel and sharp sand can also be used in the battle against heavy soil. When added to clay, these fine crushed stones separate the particles of clay and allow water to drain through.

Once you have improved your soil, you will find that there is nothing more satisfying than turning a barren soil into a fertile one.

Types of Soil

Vegetables can, within reason, be grown on most soils, but, as one would expect, there is an optimum soil in which the best vegetables can be grown. Most soils can be persuaded, with varying degrees of effort, to move towards that optimum, but the starting point is often different.

ABOVE **The better the soil, the better the crops will be. Keeping the soil in good condition is the key to successful kitchen gardening.**

Clay

When they work well clay soils can be fertile, but their structure is the despair of most gardeners. Clay is heavy and the particles cling together, making the soil sticky. Clay soil compacts easily, forming a solid lump that roots find hard to penetrate and that is difficult to dig. Try not to walk on clay soils when they are wet. This tendency to become compacted and sticky means that clay soils are slow to drain, but, once drained, they "set" like concrete, becoming a hard mass. They also tend to be cold and slow to warm up, making them unsuitable for early crops.

Clay soil is not, one would think, a good basis for growing vegetables, yet many of the best gardens are on clay. Clay soils are usually rich, and all the hard effort needed in the initial stages to improve the soil will pay off in the long term.

Sandy soils

Soils that are made up of sand and silts are quite different. They have few of the sticky clay particles but are made up of individual grains that allow the water to pass through quickly. This quick passage of water through the soil tends to leach (wash) out nutrients, so the soils are often poor. But they also tend to be much warmer in winter and are quicker to warm in spring, thus making it easier to get early crops. Silts contain particles that are a bit more clay-like in texture than those found in sandy soils, and they hold more moisture and nutrients.

Both types of soil are easy to improve and are not difficult to work. Sand does not compact like clay does (although it is still not good practice to walk on beds), but silty soils are more susceptible to the impact of feet and wheelbarrows. Adding organic material can temper their insatiable thirst.

Loams

The soil of most gardeners' dreams is loam. This is a combination of clay and sandy soils, with the best elements of both. They tend to be free draining, but at the same time

BELOW **Soil that has been well worked, as the soil in this garden clearly has, is essential to the production of good crops of vegetables.**

COMMON TYPES OF SOIL

sand
Free draining and quick to warm up, but hungry and thirsty.

loam
More moisture retentive, warms quickly and works perfectly.

silt
River deposits can be sticky, but not as sticky as clay. Rich and easy to work.

clay
Heavy and often difficult to work. Slow to warm up, but fairly rich.

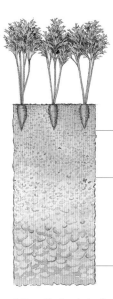

topsoil
is the dark layer of soil that contains organic material. Keep as deep as possible, although usually only one spit (spade) deep.

subsoil
is usually lighter in colour and contains little or no organic material or nutrients. It should be broken to one spit (spade) depth, but not mixed with the topsoil.

bedrock
is usually below the level of cultivation.

Soil profile A typical soil profile usually consists of three main elements: an upper layer of dark, fertile topsoil; a middle layer of lighter, infertile subsoil; and a lower layer of bedrock, which ranges from a few to hundreds of metres (yards) deep.

moisture retentive. This description – free draining and moisture retentive – is often used of soils and potting mixes and it may seem a contradiction. It means that the soil is sufficiently free draining to allow excess moisture to drain away, but enough moisture is retained for the plant without it standing in stagnant water. Such soils are easy to work at any time of the year, and they warm up well in spring and are thus good for early crops.

Acid and alkaline soils

Another way of classifying soils is by their acidity or alkalinity. Those that are based on peat (peat moss) are acid; those that include chalk or limestone are alkaline. Gardeners use a scale of pH levels to indicate the degree of acidity or alkalinity. Very acid is 1, neutral is 7 and very alkaline is 14, although soils rarely have values at the extremes of the

pH values	
1.0	extremely acid
4.0	maximum acidity tolerated by most plants
5.5	maximum acidity for reasonable vegetables
6.0	maximum acidity for good vegetables
6.5	optimum for the best vegetables
7.0	neutral, maximum alkalinity for good vegetables
7.5	maximum alkalinity for reasonable vegetables
8.0	maximum tolerated by most plants
14.0	extremely alkaline

scale. Although they can be grown on a wider range of soils, vegetables are usually grown in soils with a pH of 5.5–7.5, with the optimum conditions being around 6.5. So, the best pH for growing vegetables is slightly on the acid side of neutral. A test with a soil kit will show the rating in your own garden. You can adjust the acid soils of a garden, but it is more difficult to alter alkaline ones.

TESTING THE SOIL FOR NUTRIENTS

1 Collect the soil sample 5–8cm/2–3in below the surface. Take a number of samples, but test each one separately.

2 With this kit, mix one part of soil with five parts of water. Shake well in a jar, then allow the water to settle.

3 Draw off some of the settled liquid from the top few centimetres (about an inch) for your test.

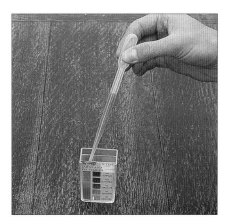

4 Carefully transfer the solution to the test chamber in the plastic container, using the pipette.

5 Select a colour-coded capsule (one for each nutrient). Put the powder in the chamber, replace the cap and shake well.

6 After a few minutes, compare the colour of the liquid with the shade panel of the container.

Improving Drainage

Few garden plants, and certainly no vegetables, like to sit in stagnant water – watercress, of course, likes water, but it must be running. A free-draining soil is of the utmost importance if you want to grow decent crops. In the majority of gardens this simply means improving the soil, but in a few gardens, where the problem is serious, it will mean installing a drainage system first.

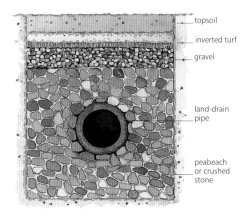

topsoil
inverted turf
gravel
land-drain pipe
peabeach or crushed stone

Section through a land drain This cross-section of a typical land drain shows the various layers of materials from which it is constructed, including the topsoil, an inverted turf or perforated plastic membrane, gravel, peabeach or crushed stone, and the land-drain pipe.

Working the soil

In many gardens wet soil can be improved simply by improving the soil itself so that the water drains away. One way to achieve this is to add organic material to improve the soil's fertility. The fibrous material contained in the organic matter helps to break up the clay particles, allowing water to pass through. This material eventually breaks down and so it should be added every time the soil is dug.

The other method is to add gravel or grit to the soil. The best material for this is what used to be known as horticultural grit – that is, grit up to about 5mm/¼in in diameter. Flint grit that has been crushed is best because the angular faces allow water to drain away better than the rounded surfaces of the uncrushed grits, such as peabeach. It may seem sacrilege to add stones to soil, but these fine gravels will make all the difference.

Drainage systems

Of course, it is no good improving the soil if the water still does not have anywhere to go. In fact, the situation could become worse because the well-drained soil in the bed could become a sump, with water running off adjacent paths and lawns into it. If water lies in the garden, then there is nothing for it but to install proper drainage. This can be a big undertaking, and many gardeners may prefer to get professional help.

The basic idea is to channel the water away from the garden. It may be possible to send it into a ditch, but under no circumstances should you connect it to the main drainage system from the house because this is bound to be breaking all kinds of local laws and regulations. If you do not have a ditch, there are two possible solutions. The first is to dig a soakaway. This is a deep hole, usually at least 2m/6ft deep, filled with clean rubble. Water runs out of the drainage pipes into the hole from which it slowly soaks away into the surrounding soil, well below the level of the beds. Alternatively, if the lay of the land allows it, excess water can be piped into a decorative pond, along with other surface water – such as that from the roof of the house, for example.

The drainage system that removes the water from the land is constructed by digging a series of trenches about 60cm/24in deep. There is one main trench, and the others join it at an angle. The trenches should slope towards the soakaway if the

LEFT **Good drainage ensures that this garden is able to support a diverse array of flowers and vegetables, including cabbages and sunflowers.**

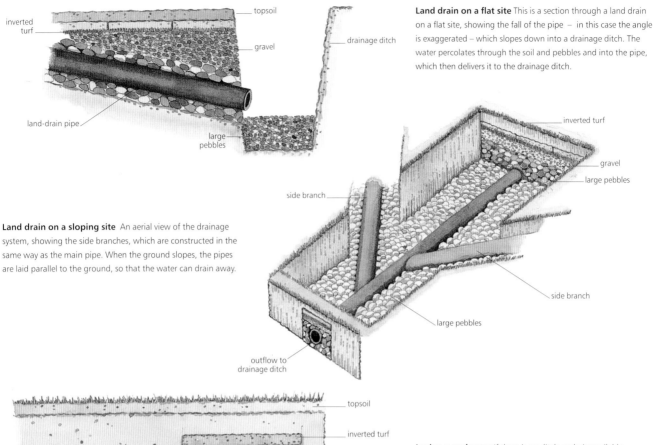

inverted turf

topsoil

gravel

drainage ditch

land-drain pipe

large pebbles

Land drain on a flat site This is a section through a land drain on a flat site, showing the fall of the pipe – in this case the angle is exaggerated – which slopes down into a drainage ditch. The water percolates through the soil and pebbles and into the pipe, which then delivers it to the drainage ditch.

inverted turf

gravel

large pebbles

side branch

side branch

large pebbles

outflow to drainage ditch

Land drain on a sloping site An aerial view of the drainage system, showing the side branches, which are constructed in the same way as the main pipe. When the ground slopes, the pipes are laid parallel to the ground, so that the water can drain away.

topsoil

inverted turf

subsoil

bricks

drainage pipe

infill of stones

Laying a soakaway If there is no ditch or drain available, then the water must be directed into a soakaway. This is a large hole filled with clean rubble or large stones. In lighter soils, it should be lined with bricks to prevent it filling with soil.

ground is flat, but should run parallel to the surface if the ground slopes. Perforated plastic tubing that comes in a continuous reel is the cheapest form of piping. This is laid on gravel with more gravel laid on top. Upturned turves are then laid on the top of the gravel (to prevent soil from washing into the gravel and blocking the drainage) and the topsoil is replaced. If turf is not available, a pervious plastic membrane can be used.

As an alternative to plastic piping, traditional tile drains can be used. These are short lengths of ceramic pipe laid with a small gap between each. A less efficient, but traditional, method is to use French drains – fill a trench with rubble and top it off with upturned turves and topsoil.

WORKING IN ORGANIC MATTER

1 Soil that has been dug in the autumn can have more organic matter worked into the top layer in the spring. Spread the organic matter over the surface.

2 Lightly work the organic material into the top layer of soil with a fork. There is no need for full-scale digging.

Soil Structure

Perhaps the most important task in any garden is to improve and maintain the quality of the soil. Good-quality soil should be the aim of any gardener who wants to grow vegetables or fruit. To ignore the soil is to ignore one of the garden's most important assets.

ABOVE **Green manure helps to improve both the structure and fertility of the soil. Sow it when the ground is not being used for anything else and then dig it in before it flowers and seeds.**

Organic material

The key to improving the soil in your garden is organic material. This is an all-embracing term that covers any vegetable matter that has been broken down into an odourless, fibrous compost. It includes such things as rotted garden waste, kitchen vegetable waste, farmyard manures (which are plant materials that have passed through animals) and other plant waste material.

It is important that any such material should be well-rotted. If it is still in the process of breaking down, it will need nitrogen to complete the process and will extract it from the soil. This, of course, is the reverse of what the gardener wants – the gardener's aim is, in fact, to add nitrogen to the soil. If you are unsure, a good indicator that the material has broken down sufficiently is that it becomes odourless. Even horse manure is free from odour once it has rotted down, and manuring a garden should not be the smelly occupation it is often depicted as being.

Some substances contain undesirable chemicals, but these will be removed if the material is stacked and allowed to weather. Bark and other shredded woody materials may contain resins, for example, while animal and bird manures may contain ammonia from urea. These chemicals will evaporate or be converted by weathering.

Digging in

The best way to apply organic material to the vegetable garden is to dig it in. In this way it becomes incorporated into the soil. If possible, double dig the bed, adding material all the way to the bottom of both spits. This will help to retain moisture and supply nutrients where they are needed, which is down by the roots. It will also encourage roots to delve deeply rather than remaining on the surface where easy water can be obtained from the odd rain shower or watering can. The deeper the roots go the more stable will be the plant's water supply and the plant will grow at a regular pace rather than in unproductive fits and starts. This will produce much better plants.

Top-dressing

Once the ground has been planted, especially with permanent vegetables and fruit, it is impossible to dig in organic material to anything more than a couple of inches. The damage done by disturbing roots makes it pointless to attempt to go any deeper. The answer here is to top-dress with well-rotted matter. A 10cm/4in layer of, say farmyard manure, will be slowly worked into the soil by the earthworms. As well as being taken into the soil, such a dressing will also act as a mulch, protecting the ground from drying out as well as preventing any weed seeds from germinating.

The top-dressing should also be free from any weed seeds or you will be creating problems rather than solving them. Properly made compost and the other types of material that can be used should always be weed free and suitable for use in this way.

Fruit and permanent plantings

For any type of plant that will be in position for several if not many years, it is important that the soil is in the best possible condition before planting begins. Once planted it will be impossible to dig in more material, and

IMPROVING SOIL FERTILITY

The fertility of the soil is much improved by the addition of organic material, but a quick boost can also be achieved by adding an organic fertilizer, spreading it over the surface and then raking it in.

REDUCING SOIL ACIDITY

The acidity of the soil can be reduced by adding lime some weeks before planting and working it in with a rake. Check the soil with a soil testing kit to see how much lime is required.

LEFT **A garden in which the soil is well cared for will reward the gardener with a plentiful harvest. In this large walled kitchen garden, rows of brassicas and espaliered fruit bushes nestle between beds planted with cosmos and marigolds.**

It is not as easy to reduce the alkalinity of soil. Peat (peat moss) used to be recommended for this purpose, but not only is collecting peat environmentally unsound, it breaks down quickly and needs to be constantly replaced. Most organic manures are on the acid side and help to bring down the levels. Leafmould, especially that from pine trees, is also acid.

Spent mushroom compost contains lime and is useful for reducing acidity, but it should not be used on chalky (alkaline) soils.

When not to add manure

Not all crops like to be grown in soil that has been freshly manured. Root crops, such as parsnips, for example, tend to "fork" when the soil is too rich. This means that, instead of the single, long, tapering roots, they have short stubby roots with several branches. The parsnip may taste the same, but it is not so convenient to clean and peel.

The way to prevent this happening is to avoid manuring before planting. Either use soil that has been manured from a previous crop – follow the brassicas, for example – or add the organic material during the previous autumn so that it has had a chance to break down before the root crops germinate and start to grow.

you will have to depend on top-dressing. Although this is a good supplement, it is not an alternative to proper preparation in the first place. The ground should be double dug if possible, and you should add as much organic matter as you can get, especially in the lower layers of soil.

Improving the soil's pH

The other aspect of improving soil is to improve the pH level. For vegetables, as we have noted, the level to aim at is pH6.5, but anything between 6 and 7 is still good, while 5.5–7.5 is acceptable.

If the soil is too acid, the pH can be adjusted somewhat by adding lime to the soil. Three types of lime can be used for reducing soil acidity. Ordinary lime (calcium carbonate) is the safest to use. Quicklime (calcium oxide) is the strongest and most caustic, but it may cause damage. Slaked lime (calcium hydroxide) is quicklime with water added; it is not as strong as quicklime and is therefore less dangerous. Always take safety precautions when you are applying lime and follow the quantities recommended by the manufacturer on the packet. Do not add lime at the same time as manure, because this will release ammonia, which can damage the plants. Spread the lime over the soil at the rate prescribed on the packet and rake it in. Do not sow or plant in the ground for at least a month. Do not over-lime.

IMPROVING SOIL STRUCTURE

1 One of the best ways to improve the structure of the soil is to add as much organic material as you can, preferably when the soil is dug. For heavy soils, this is best done in the autumn.

2 If the soil has already been dug, then well-rotted organic material can be worked into the surface of the soil with a fork. The worms will complete the task of working it into the soil.

WORKING ON WET SOIL

It is best to avoid working on wet soil, but sometimes it is necessary. To ensure that the soil is not compacted and its structure destroyed, it is advisable to work from a plank of wood.

Soil Conditioners

Quite a range of organic conditioners is available to the gardener. Some are free – if you do not count the time taken in working and carting them. Others are relatively cheap, and some, usually those bought by the bag, can be quite expensive. However, not everyone has a stable nearby or enough space to store large quantities of material, and these gardeners will therefore need to buy it as required.

Farmyard manure

A traditional material and still much used by many country gardeners, farmyard manure has the advantage of adding bulk to the soil as well as supplying valuable nutrients. The manure can come from any form of livestock, although the most commonly available is horse manure. It can be obtained from most stables, and many are so glad to get rid of it that they will supply it free if you fetch it yourself. There are often stables situated around the edge of towns, so manure is usually available to town gardeners as well as to those in the country.

Some gardeners do not like the manure when it is mixed with wood shavings rather than with straw, but it is worth bearing in mind that the former is often less likely to contain weed seeds, and as long as it is stacked and allowed to rot down it is excellent for adding to the soil as well as for use as a top-dressing.

All manures should be stacked for a period of at least six months before they are used. When it is ready, it will have lost its dungy smell.

Garden compost

All gardeners should try to recycle as much of their garden and kitchen vegetable waste as possible. In essence, this is simply following nature's pattern, where leaves and stems are formed in the spring and die back in the autumn, falling to the ground and eventually rotting and returning to the plants as nutrients. In the garden some things are removed from the cycle, notably vegetables and fruit, but as much as possible should be recirculated.

ABOVE **Farmyard manure should be left stacked in a heap until it has lost its smell and has finished rotting down.**

Compost is not difficult to make, and, of course, it is absolutely free. If you have the space, use several bins so there is always some available for use.

Unless weeds that are in seed or diseased plants have been used, compost should be safe to use as a soil conditioner and as a mulch.

Leafmould

Leafmould is a natural soil conditioner. It is easy to make and should not cost anything. Only use leafmould made by yourself; never go down to the local woods and help yourself because this will disturb the wood's own cycle and will impoverish the soil there.

SOME ORGANIC MATERIALS

well-rotted
farmyard manure

well-rotted garden
compost

Four stakes knocked into the ground with a piece of wire-netting stretched around them will make the perfect compound for making leafmould. Simply add the leaves as they fall from the trees. It will take a couple of years for them to break down and what was a huge heap will shrink to a small layer by the time the process is complete.

Add leafmould to the soil or use it as a top-dressing. It is usually acid and can be used to reduce the pH of alkaline soil. Leafmould from pine needles is particularly acid.

Peat (peat moss)

This is expensive and does little for the soil because it breaks down too quickly and has little nutritive content. It is also ecologically unsound to use it.

Spent mushroom compost

Often available locally from mushroom farms, the spent compost is relatively cheap, especially if purchased in bulk. It is mainly used in the ornamental part of the garden, but it is still useful in the vegetable garden if it is allowed to rot down. It is particularly useful if the soil is on the acid side because it contains chalk.

Vegetable industrial waste

Several industries produce organic waste material that can be useful in the garden. Spent hop waste from the brewing industry has always been a favourite among those who can obtain it. Coco shells are now imported, although these are better used as a mulch than as a soil conditioner. Several other products are locally available. Allow them to rot well before using.

Green manure

Some crops can be grown simply to be dug back into the ground to improve the soil condition and to add nutrients. They are particularly useful on light soils that are left vacant for any length of time, such as over winter.

Green manures	
Broad (fava) beans	nitrogen fixing
Italian ryegrass	quick growing
Lupins	nitrogen fixing
Mustard	quick growing
Phacelia	quick growing
Red clover	nitrogen fixing
Winter tare	nitrogen fixing

Green manures can be sown in early autumn and dug in during spring. Alternatively, if you plant fast-growing varieties, you can use them whenever land becomes available during the growing season.

Avoid letting the green manure flower and seed, otherwise it will self-seed. Most of the foliage and stems can be used in the compost bin.

BELOW **Green manure can be grown as a separate crop or it can be grown between existing crops. Here, clover is grown amongst cabbages, where it not only fixes nitrogen in the soil, but also provides a ground cover, keeping the weeds down.**

Making Compost

Compost is a valuable material for any garden, but it is especially useful in the vegetable garden. It is free, apart from any capital required in installing compost bins, but these should last a lifetime and the overall cost should be negligible. A little bit of effort is required, but this is a small price to pay for the resulting gold-dust.

The principle

The idea behind compost-making is to emulate the process in which a plant takes nutrients from the soil, dies and then rots, putting the nutrients back into the ground. In the garden, waste plant material is collected, piled in a heap and allowed to rot down before being returned to the soil as crumbly, sweet-smelling, fibrous material.

Because it is in a heap the rotting material generates heat, which encourages it to break down even more quickly. The heat also helps to kill pests and diseases as well as any weed seed in the compost. If the rotting material is to break down properly, a certain amount of moisture is needed, as well as air. If there is too much water, however, the process is slowed down; if there is insufficient air, the heap will go slimy and smell bad.

The process should take up to about three months, but many old-fashioned gardeners like to retain the heap for much longer than that, growing marrows and courgettes (zucchini) on it before they break it up for use in the garden.

The compost bin

Gardeners always seem to generate more garden waste than they ever thought possible and never to have enough compost space, so when planning your

ABOVE **A range of organic materials can be used, but avoid cooked kitchen waste or any weeds that have seed in them.** *Clockwise from top left:* **kitchen waste, weeds, shreddings and grass clippings.**

bins, make sure you have enough. The overall aim is to have three: one to hold new waste, one that is in the process of breaking down, and the third that is ready for use.

The bins are traditionally made from wood (often scrap wood), and because these can be hand-made to fit your space and the amount of material available, this is still the best option. Sheet materials, such as corrugated iron, can also be used. Most ready-made bins are made of plastic, and although these work perfectly well, they may be a bit on the small side in a busy garden.

A bin should contain at least a cubic metre/3.5 cubic feet of compost for it to heat up adequately. If you have a large garden, a bin double this size would be even more efficient. The simplest bin can be made by nailing together four wooden pallets to form a box. If the front is made so that the slats are

RIGHT **Only a small proportion of the vegetables and flowers for cutting in this plot will be used. This means that most of the foliage and stems can be put in the compost bin.**

slotted in to form the wall, they can be removed as the bin is emptied, making the job of removing the compost easier. This is a refinement, however, and not essential.

Materials

Any plant garden waste can be used for composting as long as it does not contain weed seeds. (In fact, it is useful to have a separate bin for anything that contains seeds, because the compost can be used for permanent plantings such as trees. Compost used for this purpose will never come to the surface, and any seeds will be prevented from germinating.) You should also avoid including perennial weeds. Woody material, such as hedge clippings, can be used, but shred it first.

Kitchen vegetable waste, such as peelings and cores, can be used but avoid cooked vegetables, and do not include meat, which will attract rats and other vermin.

Technique

Placing a few branches or twiggy material in the bottom of the bin will help to keep the contents aerated. Put in the material as it becomes available but avoid building up deep layers of any one material, especially grass cuttings. Mix them with other materials.

To help keep the heap warm, cover it with an old carpet or sheet of polythene (plastic). This also prevents excess water from chilling the contents as well as swamping all the air spaces. The lid should be kept on until the compost is required.

Every so often, add a layer of farmyard manure if you can get it because it will provide extra nitrogen to speed things up. Failing this, you can buy special compost accelerators. It is not essential to add manure or an accelerator, however – it just means waiting a couple of weeks longer for your compost.

Air is important, and this usually percolates through the side of the bin, so leave a few gaps between the timbers. If you use old pallets, these are usually crudely made, with plenty of gaps. The colder material around the edges takes longer to break down than that in the centre of the heap, so turn the compost around every so often. This also loosens the pile and allows air to circulate.

MAKING COMPOST

1 A simple compost bin, which should be about 1m/3ft square, can be made by nailing four flat pallets together. These bins are usually roughly made, which means that there will be plenty of air holes between the slats.

2 Pile the waste into the compost bin, making certain that there are no thick layers of the same material. Grass clippings, for example, will not rot down if the layer is too thick because the air cannot penetrate.

3 It is important to keep the compost bin covered with an old mat or a sheet of polythene (sheet vinyl or plastic). This will help to keep in the heat generated by the rotting process and it will also prevent the compost bin from getting too wet in bad weather.

4 Every so often turn the contents of the bin with a fork, partly to let in air and partly to move the outside material, which is slow to rot, into the centre so that the rotting process speeds up. It is easier if you have several bins and turn the compost from one bin into another.

5 When the bin is full, cover the surface with a layer of soil and use it to grow marrows (zucchini), pumpkins or cucumbers. If you want to use the contents as soon as possible, omit the soil and keep covered with polythene. The finished product *(inset, below)* is dark brown, crumbly and has a sweet, earthy smell, not a rotting one. It can be used straight away or left covered until required.

Fertilizers

You cannot go on taking things out of the soil without putting anything back. In nature plants return the nutrients they have taken from the soil when they die. In the garden the vegetables are removed and eaten, and the chain is broken. Compost and other organic materials help to redress the balance, but there may not be enough available to do the job properly and then fertilizers are needed.

What plants require

The main foods required by plants are nitrogen (N), phosphorus (P) and potassium (K), with smaller quantities of magnesium (Mg), calcium (Ca) and sulphur (S). They also require small amounts of what are known as trace elements, including iron (Fe) and manganese (Mn).

Each of the main nutrients tends to be used by the plant for one specific function. Thus nitrogen is concerned with plant growth and is used for promoting the rapid growth of the green parts of the plant. You should, therefore, add nitrogen to help leafy plants such as cabbage but cut back on it with plants such as runner beans, because you do not want to promote lush leaves at the expense of flowers and beans. Phosphorus, usually in the form of phosphates, is used to create good root growth as well as helping with the ripening of fruits, while potassium, in the form of potash, which is used to promote flowering and formation of good fruit, is, for example, the main ingredient in tomato feed.

The natural way

The most natural way to add nutrients to the soil is to use compost and other organic matter. As we have already seen, such materials

ABOVE **The most natural way of adding nutrients to the soil is to rot down old plant material in a compost bin, and then return it to the soil.**

are important to the general structure of the soil, but they also feed it. Well-rotted farmyard manure and garden compost have been the main way that gardeners have traditionally fed their gardens. However, some of today's gardeners are unhappy with this method because they claim that you cannot know which fertilizer you are adding and in what quantity, because the quality of organic materials varies so much. Although they concede that organic material is useful for adding bulk, they prefer to use bought fertilizers to feed the soil.

Organic material normally contains less of the main nutrients than concentrated fertilizers, but it is often strong in trace elements, and although they may not contain such a strong concentration of nitrogen, they do release it over a longer period which is of great benefit. Because of its other benefits, farmyard manure and garden compost are still the best way of treating the soil.

Organic fertilizers

Synthetic, concentrated fertilizers are broken down into two groups: organic and inorganic. Organic fertilizers are made up of chemicals derived from naturally occurring organic materials. So bonemeal (ground-up bones) is quite strong in nitrogen and phosphates,

INORGANIC FERTILIZERS

Growmore (not available in the United States)

sulphate of ammonia

potash

superphosphate

making it a good fertilizer to promote growth, especially at the start of a plant's life. Bonemeal also has the advantage in that it breaks down slowly, gradually releasing the fertilizer over a long period. When you apply bonemeal, you may want to wear gloves. Other organic fertilizers include fish, blood and bone; hoof and horn; and seaweed meal.

Because they are derived from natural products without any modification, they are deemed "safe" by organic growers.

Inorganic fertilizers

These are fertilizers that have been made artificially, although they are frequently derived from natural rocks and minerals and the process may just involve crushing. They are concentrated and are usually soluble in water. This means that they are instantly available for the plant and are useful for giving a plant a push when it is required. They do, however, tend to wash out of the soil quickly and need to be replaced.

Some are general fertilizers, and might contain equal proportions of nitrogen, phosphorus and potassium, for example. Others are much more specific. Superphosphate, for example, is entirely used for supplying phosphorus, while potassium sulphate is added to the soil when potassium is required.

ORGANIC FERTILIZERS

blood

bonemeal

seaweed

fish/blood/ bone

Increasing numbers of gardeners are turning against inorganic fertilizers, unaware that they are not as artificial as is generally believed. Many are not classified as organic simply because they are not derived from living things. Nevertheless, it is their concentrated form and the fact that they can be readily washed from the soil that lead many gardeners to object to their use.

Slow-release fertilizers

A modern trend is to coat the fertilizers so that they are released slowly into the soil. These are expensive in the short term, but because they do not leach away and do not need to be replaced as frequently, they can be considered more economic in the longer term. They are particularly useful for container planting, where constant watering is necessary (with its attendant rapid nutrient leaching).

LEFT **This kitchen garden is planted with a delightful mixture of herbs, vegetables and flowers, growing in well-fed beds.**

Digging and Breaking Down

Although it is a technique that is now being questioned by some gardeners, digging is still one of the main garden activities. It breaks up the soil, allowing the ingress of water and air, which are both important for plant growth. In addition, it also allows organic material to be incorporated deep down in the soil, right where the roots need it.

All weeds and their roots can be removed during digging, which also brings pests to the surface so that they can be destroyed. Also and importantly, it allows the gardener to keep an eye on the condition of the soil.

Single digging

The most frequently carried out method is single digging, of which there are two ways, one informal and the other formal. In the informal method the ground is usually already quite loose, and the gardener simply forks it over, turning it over and replacing it in the same position, hardly using any trench at all. This process is more frequently carried out on light or sandy soils.

Formal single digging is necessary on heavier soils and when there is organic material to be incorporated. First, a trench is dug across the width of the plot, and the earth taken from the trench is taken – in a wheelbarrow – to the other end of the bed. Compost or farmyard manure is put into the bottom of the trench and then another trench is dug. This time, the earth removed from the trench is put into the first trench to cover the organic material. This procedure is repeated down the length of the plot. When the final trench has been dug and organic material placed in it, it is refilled with the pile of soil taken from the first trench.

Further refinements can be applied. For example, the first trench can be dug so that it is two trenches wide. Dung is put in the bottom as usual, and then the next trench is dug but the soil is spread over the bottom of the previous two trenches, only half-filling them. This is then covered with another layer

ABOVE **After a winter exposed to the weather, most soils will readily break down into a fine tilth by using a rake. More recently turned soil, may need to be broken down with a heavier hoe first.**

of dung and then the fourth trench dug, filling up the first. Trenches three and four are treated in the same way, being filled first with the soil from trench five and then from trench six. This method makes a better distribution of the organic material through the soil.

Double digging

Double digging is the method that is employed to break up the subsoil, and it is useful on any new plot of ground as well as when deep beds are being prepared.

Dig the trench as before, taking the earth to the end of the plot. Then dig the soil in the bottom of the trench to the depth of a fork or spade, adding in organic material. Add more organic material on top and then dig the next trench, placing the soil into the first. Repeat until the end of the plot is reached. Take care that you do not bring any subsoil up to the top.

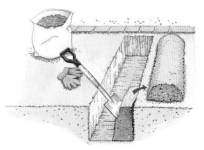

1 Start by digging a trench across the plot, putting the soil from the first trench to one side to be used later in the final trench.

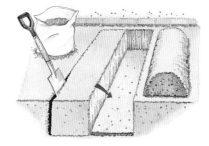

2 Put a layer of manure in the bottom of the trench. Dig out the next trench and cover over the manure in the first trench with earth taken from the second trench.

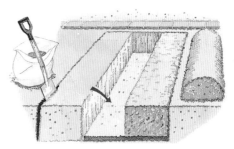

3 Repeat this process of adding manure to each trench and filling in with earth from the next, breaking up the soil as you go and keeping the surface as even as possible.

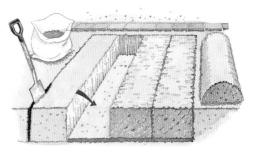

4 Continue down the length of the plot until you reach the final trench. This should be filled in with the earth taken from the first trench, which was set to one side.

DOUBLE DIGGING, METHOD ONE

1 Dig a wide trench, placing the soil to one side to be used later when filling in the final trench.

2 Break up the soil at the bottom of the trench, adding manure to the soil as you proceed.

3 Dig the next trench, turning the soil over on top of the broken soil in the first trench.

4 Continue down the plot, ensuring that subsoil from the lower trench is not mixed with topsoil of the upper.

A method requiring more energy but giving better results is to dig out the first trench and then dig another below it, keeping the two soils separate. Dig out the top spit of the next trench and also put this to one side. Add organic material to the first double trench and dig the bottom spit of the second trench into it. Add more dung and then take the top spit of the third trench and place this on top of the new soil in the bottom of the first trench. Repeat down the plot and then fill in the remaining trenches with the reserved soil from the first ones.

Mechanical digging

It is possible to dig the soil using a mechanical rotavator (rototiller). These are, however, best used on large plots. One disadvantage of using a mechanical digger is that it cuts up weed roots into small pieces, and they are more difficult to remove by hand than with conventional digging.

Breaking down into a fine tilth

The best time to dig a heavy soil is in the autumn, then the winter frosts and rain will break it down for you. If clay soils are dug in the spring and allowed to dry out too much, they are difficult to break down because the clods set like concrete. A mechanical rotavator makes breaking the soil down easier, especially if the plot is large. For smaller plots, work on the soil when it is neither too wet nor too dry (experience will show you when), breaking it down, first with a large hoe and then with a rake. Shuffling along the surface with your feet will also help considerably, but do not do this if the ground is wet.

It is better to leave sandy soils until the spring because these do not need much breaking down. Raking the surface is usually all that is required.

Occasionally, the soil becomes too hard to break down. If this happens, water the soil with a sprinkler, leave it to dry slightly – so

ABOVE **For larger gardens with heavy soil, a rotavator (rototiller) will break down the soil into a fine tilth. Even a small one saves a lot of time, especially if the soil is too dry to break down with a rake.**

that it is no longer muddy – and then break it down. Alternatively, draw out a deep sowing row in the rough soil and fill it with potting compost (soil mix) and dig this in.

DOUBLE DIGGING, METHOD TWO

1 Keeping soil from each level separate, dig first trench two spits deep. Fork over trench. Dig second trench one spit deep.

2 Add organic material to the first double trench and dig the lower spit of the second trench into it.

3 Dig an upper third trench one spit deep, and place the soil on top of that already placed in the first trench.

4 Continue, ensuring topsoil and subsoil do not mix. Fill in remaining trenches with soil taken from first ones.

techniques

There are almost as many different ways of doing things in the garden as there are gardeners. In truth, no one way is better than any other – it depends very much on who is doing what and where it is being done. Something that works for you may not help a gardener just a few doors away down the road.

Having said that, there is a certain amount of common ground in most of the techniques used in the vegetable garden, and the procedures we discuss here should stand you in good stead, even if you eventually develop your own methods. In this section you will find helpful advice on general kitchen gardening techniques, including sowing seed, both outdoors and under glass; thinning and transplanting seedlings; and harvesting and storing. There is also guidance on the cultivation of herbs, from initial planting to final drying as well as on growing, supporting and pruning fruit trees and bushes.

Sowing in the Open

Most vegetables and herbs can be sown directly into the open ground. The two main advantages of doing this are that no indoor facilities are required and the plants' growth is not delayed when they are planted out. Some plants also resent their roots being disturbed.

ABOVE **Some seed, beetroot (beets) in particular, benefits from an hour's soaking in tepid water before sowing.**

Soil requirements

The main requirement is that the soil should be broken down into a fine tilth – in other words, the soil crumbs should be small. The soil should be neither too wet nor too dry. If it is wet, cover it with cloches or polythene (plastic) to prevent it being further wetted and wait until it dries out a little before sowing. If the soil is too dry, then water the ground a short time before sowing; there should be sufficient water to soak in but not leave a sticky surface. The ground should also be warm. Seeds sown in cold ground will frequently just sit there until they rot. Ideally, the soil should be at a temperature of at least 7°C/45°F.

Seed requirements

Most of the seed that is available these days is of a high quality, especially when it comes from the major suppliers. The germination rate is usually good, although occasionally one gets an unsatisfactory batch. Non-germination, however, is usually due to some other factor, such as cold conditions. It is possible to keep your own seed, but only do this for non-F1 hybrids because F1s will not come true to type. Most seed is sold loose in packets, but seeds can be bought in other forms, and one of the most common is pelleted, when the seeds are coated with clay. The coating makes the seeds easier to handle and to sow. Increasingly, pre-germinated seeds and young seedlings are also becoming available. For most purposes, however, ordinary seeds will be suitable and certainly the cheapest.

Sowing in rows

The conventional way of sowing seeds is to do so in rows. Using a garden line for guidance, draw out a shallow drill in the fine soil with the corner of a hoe. If the ground is dry, water along the drill with a fine-rose watering can. Sow the seeds thinly. Mark the ends of the row with a label and a stick and draw the soil back over the drill with a rake. The

LEFT **Vegetables that are usually planted out, rather than sown where they are to grow, such as these cabbages, can still be sown in the open and then transplanted when they are large enough.**

SOWING SEED

1 Draw out a shallow drill with the corner of a draw hoe, using a garden line to ensure that it is straight.

2 If the soil is dry, water along the length of the drill and allow it to drain before sowing seed.

3 Sow the seed along the drill, sowing it as thinly as possible to reduce the amount of thinning necessary.

4 Put a label at the end of the row clearly showing what is in the row. Put a stick or another label at the far end. Do this before filling in the drill.

5 Rake the soil into the drill over the seed. Gently tamp down the soil along the row with the flat of the rake and then lightly rake over.

6 If the soil is heavy and is difficult to break into a fine tilth, draw out the drill and then line it with potting compost (soil mix).

depth of the drill depends on the size of the seeds, but most finer seeds should be sown at a depth of 1cm/½in. The seed packet usually gives the depth required.

Station sowing

With plants that grow quite large and therefore need to be spaced out in the row, it is wasteful to sow a continuous line of seeds. Station sowing involves sowing three seeds at distances that will be the eventual gap between plants – parsnip seeds, therefore, are sown at 20cm/8in intervals.

Wide rows

Some seeds, mainly peas and beans, are sown in wide rows – in effect, two rows are sown at once. A wide drill, 15cm/6in across, is made with the flat of the hoe. Two rows of peas or beans are sown, one down each side of the drill, and the soil is carefully raked back over the seeds so that they are not disturbed.

Broadcasting

This is the best method for sowing seeds in blocks. Rake the area to a fine tilth and scatter the seeds thinly but evenly over the surface. If the soil is dry, gently rake the seeds in and water with a fine-rose watering can.

Protecting

Fine earth is attractive to both birds and animals as a dust bath as well as a litter tray, and when it is used the seeds will be scattered far and wide. In addition, some birds find emerging seedlings an irresistible source of food. Protect the seeds by placing wire-netting guards along the rows. Alternatively, a few pea-sticks can be laid across the surface of the soil. Another possibility is to place short sticks in the ground and to twine cotton between them. This last method is the least convenient because the protection cannot be quickly removed and replaced to permit for hoeing and weeding.

Labelling

Before covering the seed with soil, mark the end of the rows with pegs and a label. Once the drill is filled in, it is difficult to see where it is. It may be some time before the seedlings emerge and the row can be easily disturbed by, for example, accidentally hoeing through it. Similarly, it is important to know what is sown where, so a label bearing the name and variety of the vegetable is important. Traditionally, many gardeners spike the seed packet on a peg but these quickly deteriorate and often blow away.

Sowing under Glass

Germinating seeds under glass is more tedious and time-consuming than sowing direct into the ground, but raising plants in this way has its advantages. It allows the gardener to grow reasonably sized plants that are ready to set out as soon as the weather allows, stealing a march on those sown in the soil by about two weeks. If there are pest problems, such as slugs or birds, the plants are better able to resist them if they are well grown when they are planted out than if they have to fight for their life as soon as they emerge through the soil.

ABOVE **There is a range of pots and trays now available that are suitable for sowing vegetable and herb seed.** *Clockwise from top left*: **individual cells or modules, a half tray, plastic pots, a fibrous pot and fibrous modules.**

Containers

Seeds can be sown in a variety of containers. Traditionally they were sown in wooden trays or flats. Some gardeners prefer to make their own, claiming that they are warmer and that they can be made deeper than the purchased equivalents. Plastic trays have, however, generally replaced the wooden varieties. They can be made of rigid plastic for multiple use or thin, flimsy plastic, and these are used only once before being thrown away.

Often, only a few plants may be required, and it is rather wasteful to sow a whole or half tray. A 9cm/3½in pot is usually sufficient.

More and more gardeners are using modular or cellular trays, in which one or two seeds are sown in a small cell. If both germinate, one is removed and the remaining seedling is allowed to develop without having to be pricked out. This method avoids a lot of root disturbance.

Even less root disturbance occurs if the seeds are sown in biodegradable fibrous modules. As soon as the seedling is big enough to be planted out, both pot and plant are inserted into the ground, and the pot allows the roots to grow through its sides into the surrounding earth.

Propagators

Propagators are glass or plastic boxes that help to keep the seed tray moist and in a warm atmosphere. The more expensive models have heating cables in them so that the temperature can be controlled. Although they are

desirable, they are by no means absolutely necessary. Cheap alternatives can also be made simply by slipping the tray into a

polythene (plastic) bag and removing it as soon as the seeds have germinated. Plastic jars can also be cut down to fit over trays or pots.

SOWING IN BLOCKS

Fill the cellular block with compost (soil mix) and tap it on the table to firm it down. Sow one or two seeds in each cell. Cover with a light dusting of compost. Remove the weaker of the two seedlings after germination.

SOWING IN TRAYS

1 Fill the seed tray with seed compost (soil mix) and tamp down the compost lightly to produce a level surface. Sow the seed thinly across the compost.

SOWING IN POTS

Fill the pot with a good seed compost (soil mix), tap it on the bench and sow one to three seeds in each pot. Once germinated, the weaker seedlings will be removed, leaving one to grow on.

2 Cover with a thin layer of compost (soil mix), lightly firm down and label. Labelling is very important because the seedlings of many vegetables look the same.

WATERING IN

Water the trays or pots by standing them in a shallow tray or bowl of water so that the water comes halfway up the container. Remove the tray or pot as soon as the surface of the compost (soil mix) begins to moisten.

Heat

A source of heat is useful for the rapid germination of seeds. It can be provided in the form of a heated propagator, but most seeds will germinate in the ambient temperature of a warm greenhouse or conservatory, or even within the house.

Sowing seed

Fill the seed tray with a good quality seed or potting compost (soil mix). Gently firm down and sow the seeds thinly on the surface. Spread a thin layer of potting compost over the seeds so that they are just covered. Again, firm down lightly. Water by placing the seed

USING A PROPAGATOR

1 Place the seeds in a propagator. You can adjust the temperature of heated propagators like this. Seed packets should indicate the best temperature, but you may need to compromise if different seeds need different temperatures.

tray in a shallow bowl of water, so that the level of the water comes halfway up the sides of the seed tray. Once the surface of the compost shows signs of dampness, remove the tray and place it in a propagator or in a polythene (plastic) bag. A traditional alternative – and one that still works well – is to place a sheet of glass over the tray.

Subsequent treatment

As soon as the seeds begin to germinate, remove the lid from the propagator – or open the bag, depending on the method you are using – to let in air and after a couple of days remove the tray altogether. If you are

2 This propagator is unheated and should be kept in a warm position in a greenhouse or within the house. Start opening the vents once the seeds have germinated to begin the hardening-off process.

using a propagator, turn off the heat and open the vents over a few days and then remove the tray.

Once the seedlings are large enough to handle, prick them out into trays, individual pots or modules. Hold the seedlings by the seed-leaves and not by the stem or roots. Make sure they are well spaced in the trays – at least 5cm/2in apart – and keep them warm and watered.

As the time approaches to plant them out, gradually harden them off by exposing them to outdoor conditions for a little longer each day until they can be safely left out overnight. They are then ready to plant out.

USING A COLD FRAME

1 Once the trays of seedlings or pricked-out seedlings are ready to plant out, harden them off by placing in a cold frame which is opened a little wider each day to let in more air.

2 Finally leave the lights of the cold frame off altogether so that the plants become accustomed to outside light.

Thinning and Transplanting

Outdoor-sown seedlings inevitably grow too thickly, no matter how thinly you try to sow them. In order to grow properly, they will need thinning. Seeds are often sown in a row that will not be their ultimate cropping position. Leeks, for example, are grown in a seed row and later transplanted to their final positions.

Why thin?

It is important that vegetables have enough space in which to develop. Plants that are too close together become drawn as they try to move to the light. In addition to not having room to develop, they become undernourished as they compete with their neighbours for moisture, nutrients and light.

Crops that are too tightly planted are more susceptible to disease because air cannot circulate freely around them, allowing fungal diseases, such as mildew, to get a hold. Half-starved plants are also more prone to disease than fully nourished ones. A little attention at this stage will pay dividends in producing healthy plants.

Thinning distances
Beetroot (beets) 7.5–10cm/3–4in
Broad (fava) beans 23cm/9in
Carrots 7.5cm/3in
Dwarf French (bush green) beans 20cm/8in
Florence fennel 25cm/10in
Kohl rabi 20cm/8in
Lettuce 23cm/9in
Parsley 15cm/6in
Peas 5cm/2in
Parsnips 15–20cm/6–8in
Radishes 2.5–5cm/1–2in
Runner beans 25–30cm/10–12in
Salsify 15cm/6in
Scorzonera 15cm/6in
Spinach 15cm/6in
Spring onions (scallions) 5cm/2in
Swedes (rutabagas or yellow turnips) 30cm/12in
Swiss chard 30cm/12in
Turnips 15cm/6in

Thinning

The idea behind thinning is to remove all unwanted plants, leaving the best at regular intervals. Before you begin to thin, water the row to soften the earth and to make sure that the remaining plants have taken up enough water in case their roots are accidentally disturbed. Allow the water to soak in and the plants to take it up. If possible, water the evening before you plan to thin.

Go along the row, with a measuring stick if you are uncertain about the distances between the plants, removing the weaker seedlings and leaving one strong one at the correct planting distance for that variety – 15–20cm/6–8in for parsnips, for example. When you pull out the unwanted seedlings, gently press the ground around the one that is left so that the pulling motion does not disturb that one as well.

When the row is complete, gently water along its length so that soil is washed back around the roots of the remaining plants that may have been disturbed. Dispose of the unwanted seedlings on the compost heap.

Avoid thinning during hot or windy conditions because the remaining plants may become desiccated before their roots can become re-established if they have been disturbed. A slightly damp, overcast day is ideal.

In hot dry weather, you can snip the unwanted seedlings off with a pair of scissors so you do not disturb their neighbours' roots.

THINNING AND TRANSPLANTING SEEDLINGS

1 Water the row of seedlings, the night before if possible, but at least a few hours before transplanting.

2 Using a hand fork, dig up, rather than pull out, the excess plants. Only dig up the plants as you need them; do not dig them up all at once and leave them lying around.

3 Using a garden line to keep the row straight, and a measuring stick to get the distances equal, replant the seedlings using a trowel.

4 Gently firm in each plant and water around them. Rake the soil around the plants in order to tidy it up and to remove footprints and uneven soil.

RIGHT **Thinning vegetables to the correct distances ensures healthy, full-sized plants: shown are rows of onions, beetroot (beets), potatoes, carrots, spinach.**

Transplanting

Plants for transplanting can either be grown from seed sown in pots or trays, or from seed sown directly in the open ground. Seedlings that have been grown in containers should be pricked out first into individual pots, or widely spaced trays, so that each plant has room to develop. Harden them off if they have been grown under glass before transplanting them into the open ground.

Damp, overcast weather conditions are ideal for transplanting seedlings because the plants will not dry out quickly in a muggy atmosphere. Again, as with thinning, it is essential to water the plants first before transplanting them. This will give them sufficient moisture to keep them going until they have re-established their root systems.

Dig up just a few plants at a time – there is no point in leaving plants lying around on the ground where they can dry out. Discard any that are weak or undernourished, and never use any that are diseased. Using a line to make sure that the row is straight and a measuring stick in order to get the planting distances correct, plant at the same depth as in the seed bed, except where stated under individual vegetables – leeks, for example, are planted deeper. Gently firm in around each plant and water in.

THINNING SEEDLINGS IN SITU

When thinning a row of seedlings that have been sown in situ, water the row the night before or at least a few hours before. Remove the unwanted plants, leaving the recommended gap between each retained plant. Try not to disturb the plants that are left. Water the seedlings after thinning and remove all the discarded seedlings to the compost heap.

USING A DIBBER

Cabbages (shown here), onions and leeks are planted out using a dibber. This makes a hole in the ground into which the plant is slipped before the earth is firmed in around it.

Planting distances

Asparagus 30–38cm/12–15in
Aubergines (eggplants) 60cm/24in
Broccoli 60cm/24in
Brussels sprouts 50–75cm/20–30in
Cabbages 30–50cm/12–20in
Calabrese (Italian sprouting broccoli) 15–23cm/6–9in
Cauliflowers 50–75cm/20–30in
Celeriac (celery root) 30–38cm/12–15in
Celery 23–30cm/9–12in
Courgettes (zucchini) 60cm/24in
Cucumbers 60cm/24in
Garlic 15cm/6in
Globe artichokes 75cm/30in
Jerusalem artichokes 30cm/12in
Kale 60cm/24in
Leeks 15cm/6in
Marrows (zucchini) 60cm/24in
Onion sets 10cm/4in
Peppers 45–60cm/18–24in
Potatoes 30–38cm/12–15in
Pumpkins 90–180cm/36–72in
Rhubarb 75–90cm/30–36in
Runner beans 25–30cm/10–12in
Seakale 30cm/12in
Shallots 15–18cm/6–7in
Sweet corn (corn) 30cm/12in
Tomatoes 60cm/24in

Harvesting and Storing

The great moment comes when the vegetables are ready to harvest; nothing tastes quite like fresh vegetables that you have grown for yourself. However, not all the produce can be eaten at once and it is prudent to store some, especially for the winter months when fresh vegetables are at a premium.

ABOVE **Harvest root crops by levering up the root with a fork and pulling on the stems or leaves.**

Harvesting

Try to resist the temptation to harvest vegetables too soon. Until they have developed fully, their taste might not be matured and some might even be bitter. Traditionally, parsnips, celery and Brussels sprouts should not be harvested until they have experienced at least one frost, which makes them taste sweeter. There are some plants that can be harvested prematurely, however, in particular leafy crops. For example, young turnip tops are worth eating, while the tips of broad (fava) bean shoots can be tasty, long before the beans themselves have matured.

When you are harvesting do not simply pick the best vegetables. If you also come across any that are diseased or rotting, harvest these as well and compost them. Do not leave rotting vegetables on the plant or in the ground because they will spread their problems to healthy fruit or the spores may remain in the ground until the following year.

ABOVE **Some vegetables are harvested by cutting through the stems as and when they are required. Swiss chard, shown here, is a good example of this method of harvesting. The stem is cut close to the base. Some gardeners prefer to twist or snap the stems off at the base rather than cutting them.**

RIGHT **Quite a number of vegetables are picked. This usually entails snapping or cutting the stem just above the vegetable so that either part of the stalk remains or there is a complete break at the junction between vegetable and stalk. Here, runner beans are being harvested.**

There is no hard and fast rule about when or at what time of day to harvest, although taking the vegetable straight from the garden to the pot does, of course, give the freshest tasting dish. If possible, try to harvest when you want a vegetable, rather than leaving it lying around for a few days before using.

Storing

There are several ways of storing vegetables for later use. If you pick or dig up a vegetable and are unable to use it right away, it can usually be kept a few days before use. The best way of keeping these is to store them in a cool, dark place, preferably a cellar or cold shed. However, this is not always possible and a refrigerator is the next best thing.

The traditional way of storing root crops throughout winter is to dig them up, clean off any dirt and remove the leaves. Then they can be placed in trays of just-moist peat (peat moss or peat substitute) or sand. The vegetables are covered with more peat and, if the tray is deep enough, another layer of root crops is placed on top and again covered in peat. Carrots, beetroot (beets), celeriac (celery root), turnips, swedes (rutabagas or yellow turnips) and parsnips can all be stored in this way.

STORING ROOT CROPS

1 Most root crops can be stored in trays of just-moist sand or peat (peat moss or peat substitute). Place a layer of peat in the bottom of the tray and then lay a row of carrots on top. Cover these with more peat.

2 Place another layer of carrots on top and cover these with more peat. Repeat with more layers until the tray is full, topping off with a layer of peat.

Unless the weather is extremely cold, parsnips, celeriac (celery root), swedes (rutabagas or yellow turnips), carrots and beetroot (beets) can simply be left in the ground until they are required. However, if a deep frost is likely to occur, it is best to lift at least a few and store them inside because it is difficult to get them out of the ground once it has frozen. Although not strictly a root crop, leeks can also be left in the ground until they are needed.

Trays of root crops should be stored in a cool, but frost-free, shed or cellar. This is also one of the best places to store many other vegetables. Squashes, pumpkins and marrows (zucchini) can be stored on shelves or wire racks. Bulbous onions, shallots and garlic can be kept in trays or in net sacks. The important thing about storing all these vegetables is that they should not touch one another and that air should be able to circulate freely around them.

Brassicas are not so easy to store, but some of the solid cabbages can be harvested and hung in nets or placed on shelves in the same cool, frost-free shed until they are required. Stored in this way, they will stay sound for several months. Some brassicas are winter hardy and can be left where they are until required. Brussels sprouts are a good example of this.

Many vegetables will freeze reasonably well. To maintain good flavour they should first be blanched (placed in boiling water) for a few minutes, the length of time depending on the type of vegetable. Details can be found in good cookery books.

Although some vegetables do not freeze well this way, many can still be frozen, simply by cooking them first – Florence fennel, for example, can be cooked and puréed before freezing.

Another, more traditional way to store vegetables and fruit is to turn them into chutneys, pickles or some other sort of preserve. Fruit is delicious when bottled.

LEFT **Many vegetables, such as these marrows (zucchini), can be stored in trays. It is best if they are not touching one another.**

Planting Herbs

There is no basic difference between planting herbs and planting vegetables. However, since herbs are often grown in their own beds it is worth considering them separately. Even if you do not have the space to grow vegetables, it is usually possible to find at least a little room for a few herbs.

ABOVE **Plants such as mint that spread rapidly underground should be planted in a large bucket or flowerpot, about 30cm/12in across or more, which is then sunk into the ground. The rim of the pot should be level with the surface of the soil.**

Siting herbs

There are many reasons for growing herbs. They can be purely decorative or they can be medicinal, but within the context of this book they are culinary. Herbs for the kitchen are usually required instantly, with the cook dashing out in the middle of cooking to grab a handful, and so the most convenient site for this type of herb is as close to the kitchen door as possible. From a horticultural point of view, most herbs like to be in an open, sunny position.

Soil preparation

Herbs will grow in the same soil you have in your vegetable garden, and, like vegetables, they prefer a rich, moisture-retentive soil. Dig and prepare the ground thoroughly, adding plenty of well-rotted organic material. At the same time, remove any perennial weeds. This is particularly important around permanently planted herbs, such as chives, mint and sage, because there will not be an easy opportunity for removing the weeds if they reappear.

Sowing

Some herbs, such as parsley, can be sown directly into the ground. This makes a great deal of sense if you want to have a whole row or block of them. However, make sure that the soil is warm enough before you plant. In cold springs, wait until the soil warms up first, even if it means missing the theoretical first sowing date. For example, parsley will not germinate if the soil is too cold, and you will have to re-sow because the first sowing of seeds will invariably rot. Thin the resulting seedlings to the appropriate distances.

For small quantities of herbs or in cold springs, it is a good idea to sow the herbs under glass and plant them out once they are big enough. They can be sown in modules to reduce the amount of root disturbance. Thoroughly harden off before planting out.

Planting

When you are planting out, remember that herbs need space to grow and you should allow for their increase in size. This is particularly important with shrubby plants such as sage and rosemary, which can grow from small cuttings when first planted out to up to 1.2m/4ft or more across. In addition, when you are deciding what to plant where, put the taller ones to the north so that they do not overshadow the smaller ones.

Plant the herbs at the same depth in the soil that they were in their pots. Gently firm them in, water and tidy up the soil to remove footprints. Loosen the soil if it is compacted.

Wayward herbs

Some herbs, mint in particular, are rampant. If they are planted in a bed they will rapidly spread and soon invade other, nearby

LEFT **Some time before planting, give the plant a thorough soaking.**

PLANTING OUT

1 Using a trowel, dig a hole in the prepared ground that is slightly larger than the rootball of the plant.

2 Insert the plant so that the top of the rootball is level with the surface of the soil. Fill in the hole around the plant and firm down.

3 Water the plant and the soil immediately surrounding the rootball.

plants. One way to cope with this is to plant the mint in a bottomless bucket or large plastic flowerpot. Dig a large hole and then place the bucket or flowerpot into it so that the rim is level with the surface of the soil. Fill the bucket or flowerpot with the excavated soil and fill in the remaining hole around the edge of the pot with the rest of the soil. Plant the mint in the centre of the container and water. The questing roots will now be prevented from moving far because of the walls of the pot. Since the roots do not grow far down, they will not be able to exit through the bottom of the bucket or the holes in the pot, which will permit free drainage so that the container does not become waterlogged. Containers used in this way will become congested, and a piece of the mint should be replanted with fresh soil every year. Planting mint in a corner that is confined by paths is another way of keeping it in check.

ABOVE **Planting herbs next to a path means that the delightful scent of fresh herbs is released when someone brushes past them.**

Growing Herbs in Containers

Containers are the perfect way to ensure that herbs are in just the right amount of light or shade. The mature herbs can later be transferred to the garden, or kept conveniently close to hand in their pots on a patio or kitchen window sill. Planting in pots also gives scope for adding height and depth to a border, and a group of pots can form an attractive garden feature or balcony arrangement.

ABOVE **Herbs can be planted in a variety of containers. This wooden box has useful handles for moving the herbs to different locations.**

Choosing pots

Herbs can be grown in any form of container – even old coleslaw cartons, ice-cream cartons or plastic picnic boxes – but they will always look better and more at home if you choose an attractive container that has been properly designed for growing plants.

There are plenty to choose from – nurseries and garden centres stock them by the hundred – and they are no longer as expensive as they once were. Always try to choose one that is big enough for your needs.

Remember that plants need room to spread out their roots if they are to grow well and remain healthy, and if you are intending to grow several different types of herb you will need a large pot or several of them.

The shape does not matter too much as long as you do not choose an Ali Baba type pot, with a bulbous belly and a narrow neck, because the opening will not be large enough to get many herbs in (although such a pot could look beautiful with a single sage). Pot-bellied shapes work well if they

are designed like strawberry pots with openings in the side to take individual herbs. Window-boxes also make good herb containers. They can be used on the ground or mounted outside the kitchen window or simply on a nearby wall.

Whatever type of container you choose, make certain that it has drainage holes in the bottom so that excess water can drain away.

Planting the herbs

If the container is large, it is likely to be heavy once it is full of damp compost (soil mix), so, if possible, position it before you fill it. Cover the bottom of the container with irregularly shaped stones to help any excess water find its way to the drainage holes. Fill the pot with a good quality compost and firm this down lightly. Then plant the herbs, making sure that they are the same depth as they were in their original pots. Smooth over the top of the compost and

LEFT **Mints are very rampant, so it is a good idea to grow them in pots. Here, a selection of mints is growing in terracotta pots.**

adjust the level of the surface, removing or adding some to bring it just below the rim of the container. Water herbs thoroughly.

Maintenance

The biggest task is to keep the herbs well-watered. During the summer months, when it is hot and dry, the container is likely to need watering at least once a day and even twice a day in some circumstances. All this watering means that nutrients quickly leach from the soil, so it will be necessary to add a liquid feed to the watering at least once a week. As an alternative, a slow-release fertilizer can be added to the potting compost (soil mix) before the container is filled.

Re-potting

Herbs will not last forever in a container, and if you are to be sure of a continuous supply it will be necessary to re-pot at least once a year. Many herbs are best thrown away and new ones planted in any case, and this applies even to perennials. Sage and rosemary will eventually get large, and it is better to replace these with new plants every year or every second year at the most, unless you have a container large enough to keep them for longer.

Always wash out a container thoroughly and refill it with new compost (soil mix), adding the old soil to the vegetable garden.

ABOVE **Even if you only have a small garden, you can still make room for a large container planted with culinary herbs.**

PLANTING HERBS IN A CONTAINER

1 To ensure that no stagnant water lies in the bottom of the container, place a layer of irregularly shaped stones in the bottom. This will ensure good drainage.

2 Fill the container with a good potting compost (soil mix). Firm it down gently.

3 Plant the herbs by digging holes in the compost (soil mix) and then firming them in. Top up or reduce the amount of compost so that it is just below the rim of the container.

4 To ensure that the plants are kept fed, insert one or more fertilizer sticks into the compost, following the manufacturer's instructions on the packet.

5 Water the container thoroughly and place in the shade for a few days until the herbs have recovered and become established.

Harvesting and Storing Herbs

Many herbs are seasonal and are not available for cutting all year round. One way of overcoming this problem is to grow some indoors, where they will survive the winter, but this is not always convenient and a better solution is to dry and store as many different types of your herbs as you can.

ABOVE **Harvest herbs when they are at their peak, usually before they flower. Cut them on a dry day, avoiding times when they are wilting in the heat.**

Harvesting herbs

Many herbs, such as parsley, rosemary and sage, are harvested on a cut-and-come-again principle: you take just as much as you want, when you want. With care, you can have parsley all year round. Sage and rosemary, being evergreen shrubs, should present no problems. Most other herbs, however, die back in winter and are not available unless you harvest and store them.

The time to pick herbs for storing is when they are fresh and at their peak, and with most herbs this is before they come into flower. (This, of course, applies to leaf herbs; if you want the seeds, obviously you must let the plants flower.) If you wait until after flowering, the leaves on most herbs will be tired, and will have lost their freshness and lack the sweetness of younger plants. On some plants the lower leaves are best avoided, because these are old and past their best.

Avoid gathering herbs in the heat of the day, when the leaves may be limp. If you can, work early in the morning, as soon as any dew has disappeared. Do not harvest on wet days. It is easier to dry herbs if the whole stem is collected, so cut neatly with a pair of secateurs (pruners). Pick flowers on warm, dry days when they have just fully opened.

Seeds should also be collected on dry days and should be fully ripe before they are harvested. Tip the seeds into a paper bag or place the whole seedhead in the bag.

Root herbs, such as horseradish, should be harvested in autumn, once the above-ground parts begin to wither.

Drying herbs and flowers

The simplest way to dry any type of herb is to tie the stalks in small bunches and hang them in a warm, dark place where plenty of air can circulate. Although they can be hung in a light place, including indoors, do not place them in direct sunlight. An airing cupboard or a warm room is best, but kitchens and bathrooms, where there is a lot of steam, are not suitable. Do not put herbs into an oven, because they will dry too quickly. Individual leaves can be dried by placing them on mesh trays or sheets of muslin or on ordinary trays. Those with a mesh are preferable because air will circulate more freely around the leaves.

Do not dry different herbs in close proximity or you may find that they taint each other.

DRYING AND FREEZING HERBS

1 Pick seed just as it is ripening. At this stage it should readily come away from its stalks. Place it on a tray or muslin bag and leave the seed for a few days in a warm, dry place until it has completely dried.

2 Once herbs have been thoroughly dried, tip them into a glass jar with an airtight lid. Store in a cool, dry, dark place.

3 An alternative to drying is to freeze herbs. They can simply be packed into bags and frozen, or finely chopped and placed in ice-cube trays. Add water to the trays and freeze to produce ready-to-use cubes.

ABOVE **Oregano, which can be dried or frozen, is a useful herb for the kitchen.**

Drying roots

Roots should be cleaned and cut into small pieces and dried on a tray in the oven.

Storing

Do not attempt to store any herbs until they are completely dry. When they are dry, place them in airtight glass jars. Clear jars can be used if the herbs are to be kept in a cupboard, but dark glass is preferable for those to be left on open shelves. Keep the leaves whole if possible and crush them only just before use.

Freezing

A modern alternative to drying herbs is to freeze them. This has the advantage of keeping the plant's colour as well as being much quicker and easier to do. The cleaned herbs can be put into labelled polythene (plastic) bags and put directly into the freezer. Alternatively, the herbs can be finely chopped and placed in ice-cube trays. Add a little water to each and freeze. Individual frozen cubes can be added to dishes as required.

Infusions

Another possibility is to make flavoured oils and vinegars for using in cooking. A few sprigs of the herb are infused in a bottle of good-quality wine vinegar or in an olive or vegetable oil.

RIGHT **Herbs can be dried by tying them into bunches and hanging them in a warm, dry place such as near a stove or boiler. However, take care to avoid steamy places and direct sunlight.**

Growing Fruit Trees and Bushes

Fruit tends to be the poor relation in the garden, possibly because it can take up large amounts of space. However, fresh fruit is even more delightful than fresh vegetables and it need not take up as much space as you might think.

Where to grow your fruit

The traditional place to grow fruit is in a fruit garden, a separate area of the garden that is devoted to fruit. This has one especial advantage in that it can be completely protected in a fruit cage. Scattering the fruit over the whole garden means that individual plants have to be protected, which can be rather tedious.

Apart from the protection they require, however, there is no reason for keeping the fruit together. In a decorative kitchen garden, fruit can be mixed in with the vegetables, trees and standard bushes providing visual height in individual beds. Many fruit trees can also be grown along walls or fences, and they can be used as dividers or screens between various parts of the garden. If you have a small garden and

want a shady tree to sit under, why not plant an apple tree rather than a species that is solely ornamental?

Choosing fruit

As long as it will grow in your garden, there is nothing to prevent you choosing whatever fruit you want. There is a slight complication in that some tree fruits need pollinators to make sure that the fruit is set, and this means that if you want a particular apple you may have to have another apple to act as a pollinator. This may not be necessary if your neighbour has a compatible tree.

Ground preparation

Most fruit trees and bushes are likely to remain in the ground for a long time and so it is important that the soil is thoroughly prepared. It is particularly important that all perennial weeds are removed. If any small piece is left in the ground it is bound to regrow and is likely to be difficult to extract from around the roots of the tree or bush without digging them up.

Another reason for preparing the ground thoroughly is to make sure that there is plenty of organic material tucked right down among the roots of the plants. This will help keep the soil moist as well as giving a continuous supply of nutrients until the plants are established. Once the tree and shrubs are planted, any organic material will have to be applied to the soil's surface and taken down by the worms. Double dig the soil if possible,

ABOVE **Strawberries can be grown in containers. If these are kept under glass, as here, then an early crop can be obtained.**

incorporating as much well-rotted organic material as you can spare. Take this opportunity to make sure that all perennial weeds are removed. If the ground is heavy and it is

PLANTING A FRUIT TREE OR BUSH............

When planting a fruit tree or bush, always ensure that it is planted at the same depth as it was in its container or in its nursery bed.

TYING IN A NEWLY PLANTED TREE............

Using tree ties, ensure that a newly planted tree is firmly anchored to a stake. Attach the tie approximately 30cm/12in above the ground.

ABOVE **Even apple trees can be grown in containers. However, it is essential to water them every day, and at least twice on hot dry days.**

In the autumn, and again in the spring, top-dress fruit bushes with a layer of well-rotted organic material such as farmyard manure.

Strawberries can be grown through a black polythene (plastic) mulch. This not only protects the fruit from mud-splashes, but also reduces the need for weeding and watering.

likely to be difficult to remove the weeds, spraying some time before digging may be the only answer to cleaning the soil.

Planting

As long as the weather is neither too wet nor too cold the best time to plant fruit trees and bushes is between late autumn and mid-spring. If bare-rooted plants are delivered when it is impossible to plant, heel them into a spare piece of the vegetable garden until they can be planted in their permanent position. Container-grown plants can be planted at other times of the year, but they need more attention to make sure that they survive.

Fruit trees and bushes should be planted to the same depth as they were in their pots or nursery bed when you purchased them. If a tree needs staking, place the stake in the ground before planting. Water the plants in thoroughly and keep them watered in dry weather until they are firmly established. Apply a mulch around the base of the plant in order to help preserve moisture as well as to keep the weeds down. Remove any weeds that do appear.

Try to keep a record of what you have planted. Fruit trees and bushes often outlive any label that comes with them, and it is often annoying when asked for the variety of an apple or raspberry, for example, when you cannot remember. A notebook with details of the variety, where you purchased the plant as well as the date on which you planted it, will be of future interest.

Supporting Fruit Trees and Shrubs

Once they are established, some fruit shrubs and most trees are free-standing, but most benefit from, and some require, permanent support. If this is provided adequately and properly from the start, these supports should last many years.

Wall and fence fruit

Several types of trees and shrubs can be trained flat against walls or fences. The effects created can be decorative. These plants will need some means of holding them against the wall, and this usually takes the form of wires. To make sure that the framework lasts as long as possible use a galvanized wire, which will not corrode. The wire is held in place by vine eyes, of which there are several types available. Some are flat, metal spikes, which are hammered into the brickwork, while others are screw eyes, which are screwed into wall plugs that have been inserted into holes in the brick or stonework of the wall. They can be screwed directly into wooden fences. The eyes are placed 60–90cm/ 2–3ft apart and a wire led through the hole in each one. The wire is secured at the end eyes by pulling it back and twisting it around itself or by using a tensioning screw that can be tightened to tension the wire. The wires should be parallel to each other and 30–45cm/12–18in apart.

Free-standing wirework

Berried fruit – like raspberries, blackberries and the various hybrid berries – and grapes need a permanent framework. They are grown in the open, and it is necessary to build a

ABOVE **This apple tree is being supported by wires in a very decorative manner.**

structure that will carry the supporting wires. The end posts are the most important part of the structure because they take a strain in one direction only, and if they are not secured properly they can be pulled from the ground. Each post should be treated with a preservative to prolong its life. The end posts should be sunk into the ground by at least 60cm/ 24in and braced with another post set at an angle. Intermediate posts, every 2m/6ft or so, are set to a similar depth but do not need bracing. Galvanized wire is stretched along the length of the row, at 30cm/12in intervals, the first wire being 60cm/24in from the ground. These wires should be as taut as possible. They can be fixed with staples, or holes can be drilled in the posts and eye-bolts inserted, which can be used to tension the wire by tightening the nut on the outside of the end posts.

Individual support

Trees need individual support when they are first planted. In exposed positions some shrub fruit, especially standards, will also benefit from being supported.

SUPPORTING A TREE AGAINST A WALL

1 To support trees against walls, use wires held by vine eyes. Depending on the type of vine eye, either knock them into the wall or drill and plug before screwing them in.

2 Pass galvanized wire through the holes in the eyes and fasten to the end ones, keeping the wire as tight as possible.

The stake should be inserted before the tree is planted so that there is no chance of damaging the roots. Although the stake should be knocked well into the ground, there need only be about 45cm/18in above ground. Current practice is to support trees low down, at about 30cm/12in above the ground, so that the lower part of the tree and, more importantly, the rootball, are held in place, while the top is allowed to move freely, gaining strength as it does so.

Tie the tree to the stake, using a proper tree tie that will provide good support, but at the same time not cut into or chafe the trunk of the tree. It is important that you check at least twice a year that the tie is not too tight and cutting into the growing trunk. Adjust the tie if necessary.

If the tree is already in position, place the stake at an angle to the trunk so that it enters the ground some way from its base in order to avoid damaging the tree's roots. Alternatively, insert two posts, each some distance from, and on either side of, the trunk. Fix a crossbar between these two posts, and then tie the tree to this.

BELOW **The branches of small apple trees can be trained to spread by tying them down with string tied to the trunk.**

STAKING FRUIT

1 Knock a stout post well into the ground at the end of the row. An alternative is to dig a hole and insert the post before refilling and ramming down the earth.

2 Knock another post at a 45° angle to the vertical to act as a support to the upright post. Nail it firmly so that the upright post is rigid and will not be pulled by tight wires.

3 Fasten the wires around one end post and pull tight along the row stapling it to each post. Keep the wire as taut as possible. If necessary, use eye-bolts on the end posts to tension the wire.

4 Fasten the canes – in this case raspberry canes – to the wire with string or plant ties. Space the canes out evenly along the wire so that the maximum amount of light reaches the leaves.

Pruning Fruit Trees and Bushes

Pruning is a subject that terrifies many gardeners. Indeed, many gardeners fail to prune at all, to the detriment of the tree or the bush and to their subsequent crops. Like so many other things connected with gardening it is largely a question of experience. Once you have practised it a couple of times, you will be able to do it without any trouble at all.

Basic pruning cuts

Although trees and shrubs need different methods of pruning and training, the pruning cuts are the same in all instances. Always cut a stem just above a bud and make sure that the cut is angled away from the bud.

Branches that are large enough to be cut with a saw are usually cut across the branch at right angles. If the branch is thick and heavy and likely to break, thereby splitting the wood before the cut is complete, the sawing is done in three separate stages. The first cut is made on the underside of the branch, 5cm/2in from the final cutting position. The second cut is made slightly further out along the branch, this time from above, by sawing down until the branch splits along to the first cut and is then severed. The final cut can be made straight through from the top because there is now no weight to cause splitting.

Shapes

There are many different ways of pruning and training fruit trees and bushes, and some of the procedures are quite complex. See the box, above right, for descriptions of the most popular shapes.

Rootstocks

The rootstock on which a fruit tree grows affects the size and rate of growth of the tree. It is important that you get the right stock for the type of tree you want to grow. Always check with the supplier that the tree or bush is suitable for your needs.

ABOVE **A standard apple tree is a particularly good shape for a traditional garden. It also provides shade in the summer.**

Fruit Tree and Bush Shapes

Standard trees are full-sized trees with a natural shape. These need space as they can grow large, but they create good shade for sitting under.

Half-standard trees are similar to standard trees, but, as the name implies, they are smaller.

Bush trees are much smaller than standards but are still quite large for a small garden. The trees are quite short but bushy with an open centre.

Spindle-bush trees are short – to 2.1m/7ft high – and cone shaped, with a central leader and side branches that are tied down to make them spread.

Dwarf pyramid trees are short growing and pruned into a pyramid shape. In general, more branches are retained than in the similarly shaped spindle-bush trees.

Fan trees or bushes are trained so that the branches are in a two-dimensional fan, radiating from the top of a short trunk. They are grown against a wall, a fence or post-and-wire supports.

Espalier trees or bushes are trained flat against a wall, a fence or post-and-wire supports. They have a main trunk and parallel branches coming from it at right angles.

Cordon trees or bushes consist of a single main stem. They are usually trained at 45° to the ground, but they can be also be vertical.

Double cordon trees or bushes are similar to ordinary cordons, except two shoots are trained vertically, forming a U-shape.

Triple cordons are similar to ordinary cordons, except three stems are trained vertically.

Standard bushes are grafted onto a single tall stem to give it a "lollipop" appearance.

ABOVE **Pears are the perfect fruit to grow in all manner of decorative shapes. Here, the pear is being trained into a crown shape.**

TOP LEFT **An espaliered pear tree on wire supports. Many other fruit trees can be trained in the same decorative way.**

OPPOSITE PAGE, TOP **This pear tree has been beautifully trained into a fan. The fan is supported on wires, but it could also be grown against a wall.**

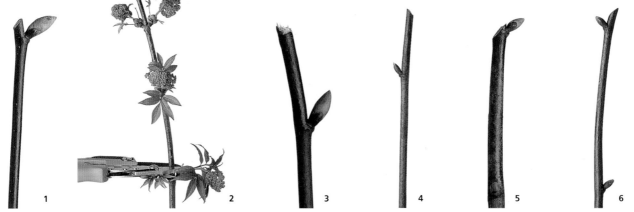

1   2   3   4   5   6

Good and Bad Pruning Cuts

1 A good pruning cut is made just above a strong bud, about 3mm/⅛in above the bud. It should be a slanting cut, with the higher end above the bud. The bud should generally be outward bound from the plant rather than inward; the latter will throw its shoot into the plant, crossing and rubbing against others, which should be avoided. This is an easy technique and you can practise it on any stem.

2 If the stem has buds or leaves opposite each other, make the cut horizontal, about 3mm/⅛in above the buds.

3 Always use a sharp pair of secateurs (pruners). Blunt ones will produce a ragged or bruised cut, which is likely to introduce disease into the plant.

4 Do not cut too far above a bud. The piece of stem above the bud is likely to die back and the stem may well die back even further, causing the loss of the whole stem.

5 Do not cut too close to the bud otherwise the bud might be damaged by the secateurs (pruners) or disease might enter. Too close a cut is likely to cause the stem to die back to the next bud.

6 It is bad practice to slope the cut towards the bud as this makes the stem above the bud too long, which is likely to cause dieback. It also sheds rain on to the bud, which may cause problems.

Protecting Fruit

Gardeners are not the only animals to like fruit. Many others, birds in particular, do so as well, and the only way to make sure that there is enough left for the gardener to enjoy is to protect the fruit bushes and trees in some way. The only practical way to do this is to put some form of physical barrier between the predators and the fruit.

ABOVE **A tunnel of wire netting can be used to protect low-growing strawberries. The netting can be in short sections for easy removal and storage.**

Fruit cages

There is no doubt that the easiest way to protect fruit is with a complete cage. The advantage of this is that it covers the area completely and that the gardener can walk around within it, maintaining the bushes or harvesting the fruit. When individual protection is provided, each cover has to be removed in turn, which can be tiresome, especially if netting snags on branches.

The only problem with caging on a large scale is that it can be expensive. If you have every intention of leaving the fruit cage where it is, it might be more economical in the long term to build a cage with long-lasting materials. Use thick posts and make the covering from galvanized wire netting, which, although more expensive than plastic, will outlive many replacements of its plastic equivalent.

Ready-made fruit cages are expensive but they still probably work out cheaper than making one of your own, unless, of course, you have access to free materials, such as posts. Fruit cages are supplied in kit form and are easy to erect; they can usually be ordered to whatever size you require. Make sure that there are no gaps in the netting and that it is well pegged down or buried at the base because birds have a knack of finding the smallest hole to squeeze through.

A homemade fruit cage is time-consuming to construct, but you can make it fit any shape and cover any area you want. Metal posts, such as scaffolding poles, will last for ever but most gardeners find that wooden poles are more practical. They should be sturdy and treated at their base with preservative. Each should be let into the ground by about 60cm/24in for security, because the netting will act as a sail, putting great pressure on the posts in strong winds.

The covering can be plastic netting, but galvanized wire netting will last longer and be less likely to tear accidentally. Some gardeners like to remove the top covering to allow birds in to eat pests when the fruit is not actually ripening, and if you want to do this, use wire sides and a plastic netting for the top. Another reason for being able to remove the top covering in winter, especially if it is plastic, is that a heavy fall of snow can

LEFT **A fruit cage is expensive but it is the only really effective way of protecting fruit from birds.**

ABOVE **Strawberries can be protected against frost with cloches.**

LEFT **Fruit trees and bushes trained against a wall or fence can be protected with a home-made frame, as seen here. A similar frame can be covered with polythene (plastic) to protect the blossom from frosts.**

Draped netting

There is no satisfactory way of protecting taller, free-growing subjects, such as fruit bushes or trees. Draping them with netting is the only possible method, but gaps are usually left and the netting snags on twigs and shoots

If a fruit is growing against a wall or fence, then the netting can be held away from the plant by building a simple frame, and this can also be covered with polythene (plastic) in the spring in order to protect the blossom against frost.

Non-netting protection

Netting is the only satisfactory way to protect fruit crops in the garden. Commercial methods, such as bangers, are impracticable in a domestic garden. Humming wires have a limited success but do not really work. Covering the bushes with threads may keep the birds off but they make harvesting awkward and they are difficult to remove for pruning.

The traditional scarecrow makes a good feature in the garden, but it has no success in deterring birds and animals. Plastic birds of prey or owls at strategic points often work well for a while, but birds soon get used to them.

stretch and break it. The tops of the poles are best covered with a smooth rounded object – the bottom of a plastic drinks bottle is ideal – and although it may look ugly, it will prevent the plastic netting from being chaffed and worn as the wind moves it against the posts.

Make a door wide enough to get a wheelbarrow through and make certain that it fits well, or birds will get in.

Low-level protection

It is easier to provide protection for individual crops when low-level protection is required because less material is needed. The simplest method is to bend some wire-netting into an inverted U-shape and peg it to the ground with wires. This works well for strawberries. Alternatively, put short stakes in the ground at intervals all round and in the middle of the crop and drape plastic netting over this.

Harvesting and Storing Fruit

The best fruit is always the crop you pick and pop straight into your mouth. Given kind weather and a certain amount of skill on the gardener's part, however, there should be sufficient fruit not only to supply the kitchen but also to store for later use.

Harvesting

Fruit should be properly ripe before it is harvested for immediate use. There is little point in picking it early and leaving it to ripen – it will always ripen better on the stem. Fruit for storing should be mature and ripe – but do not pick at the very peak of ripeness, aim for just a little before. This is a matter of judgement and will come with experience. The time to pick is when the fruit comes away easily in the hand. Apples, for example, will come free with a little twist of the wrist, while raspberries will come away when twisted with the fingers.

With the exception of cane fruit, such as raspberries and blackberries, most fruit is picked with the stalks left on. Normally fruit is picked individually, but the various types of currant and grapes are usually picked in bunches. Pick fruit during dry weather and be careful not to bruise or otherwise damage it.

Storing

On the whole, the only types of fruit that can be satisfactorily stored without some method of preservation are apples, pears and quinces, and it is worth remembering that some varieties of fruit store better than others. 'Cox's Orange Pippin' apples, for example, can be kept until spring, but 'Beauty of Bath' apples have to be eaten right away, because they last not much longer than a week. As a general rule, early maturing apples do not store, but later ones do.

ABOVE **Apples are removed with a twist of the wrist. All fruits, other than cane fruit such as raspberries and blackberries, are picked with the stalks left on.**

Keep only fruit that is in perfect condition and throw out any that are marked or beginning to rot. Place the apples or pears in trays separated with paper so that they do not touch each other. Place the trays in a cool, dark place. Check periodically and throw out any fruit that is beginning to rot. Some apples will shrivel in storage and it is better to wrap these individually in grease-proof paper or to place several in a polythene (plastic) bag that has a few small holes in it.

ABOVE AND LEFT **Soft fruit, such as strawberries, raspberries and gooseberries should be carefully picked between thumb and finger. The fruit may then be placed in small individual containers so that they are not squashed or bruised.**

RIGHT **A filbert tree (*Corylus maxima*) is a rare but welcome sight in the garden. The variety shown here is 'Purpurea'.**

Do not place quinces close to apples and pears because the strong aroma will taint the other fruit. Store quinces in open trays.

Freezing

It is possible to freeze most fruit. However, although the taste will remain, many will lose their "solid" appearance when thawed and are, therefore, better used for cooking than for eating raw. Soft fruits are the easiest to freeze, but it is also possible to freeze apples, although it is best to cut them up or even cook and purée them before freezing.

Again, only choose sound fruit. Place the fruit on trays so that they are not touching each other and then put them in the freezer. Once frozen, they can be put into a bag. The fruit can be put straight into a bag before freezing, but they are likely to stick together and so the whole batch will have to be used at once. If you have no room for trays, split the fruit up into small usable quantities and place each batch of fruit in an individual bag.

Preserving

Freezing is a modern method of preserving fruit, but there are also a number of traditional ways. Some fruits, such as apples and pears, can be dried while others, such as plums and gooseberries, can be bottled. Another way is to turn the fruit into chutneys or jams. All these methods are dealt with in good cookery books.

ABOVE **Apples, pears and quinces can be stored in trays in a cool place. It is best if they are laid on paper so that the individual fruits do not touch. The length of storage time depends on the variety.**

ABOVE **With the exception of apples, pears and quinces, most fruit cannot be kept for any length of time without some form of preserving. The simplest method of preserving fruit is to freeze it.**

Propagation

While most gardeners do not have much space to increase their stock, and many do not need to replace their tree fruit, they need to know how to propagate soft fruits, so that they can be replaced from time to time. The techniques involved are all fairly simple to master.

Hardwood cuttings

Currants, gooseberries, blueberries and grape vines are usually increased by taking hardwood cuttings. This process does not need any propagators or other equipment other than a pair of secateurs (pruners) or a sharp knife.

The best time for taking hardwood cuttings is autumn, preferably early autumn. Select a few shoots that have grown during the previous year and are now firm and well-ripened. They should be straight and about 30cm/12in long.

Choose a sheltered site, away from drying winds and hot sun. Make a narrow trench by inserting a spade into the soil and pushing it to one side to open up a narrow V-shaped slit. If the soil is heavy, trickle some clean sharp sand into the bottom of the slit and insert the cuttings. Place them about 15cm/6in apart, planting them so that about half of the cutting is below ground. Place the spade into the ground about 10cm/4in away from the initial slit and lever it so that the slit closes up, firmly holding the cuttings. Firm down the soil gently with your feet.

By the next autumn the cuttings should have rooted. They can be dug up and transplanted to their final positions or moved to a nursery bed for another year.

Layering

Blackberries and hybrid berries are best increased by the simple process of layering, as are strawberries, although the latter are usually obliging enough to do it themselves, leaving the gardener to transplant the new plants.

At some time during the growing season choose a healthy blackberry cane that is long enough to touch the ground. At the point where the tip makes contact with the soil, dig a hole about 10cm/4in deep. Place the tip in it and bury it by replacing the soil. If it is in an exposed position and it is possible that the cane will be blown or knocked out of the ground, you can secure it with a peg, although this is not normally necessary. By late autumn the tip will have rooted. Cut the new plant from its parent shoot, about 30cm/12in from the ground. Dig up the young plant and transplant it to its fruiting position.

ABOVE **This strawberry plant is producing plenty of runners, which root to produce a number of different plants.**

If you want to grow a few new plants in pots, perhaps for selling, the young plant can be transplanted directly into a pot. However, it is possible to cut out this stage by burying the tip of the parent cane into a pot of potting compost (soil mix) instead of a hole in the ground; it will root just as easily. The pot can be let into the ground, which will prevent it from being knocked over and it will not dry out as quickly as it would if left standing on the ground.

Strawberries can be treated in a similar way. After fruiting they send out runners, which will drop roots at intervals along their length to produce new plants. To make sure that they root, you can peg them down or cover a short length of runner with soil, but

LAYERING

1 Blackberries, hybrid berries and strawberries can all be increased by layering. Choose a healthy shoot, dig a hole near the tip and then bury it.

2 After a short period the tip will have produced roots. It can then be cut from the parent plant and replanted where required.

3 If you would like to have potted specimens, then bury a flowerpot in the ground, fill it with compost (soil mix) and bury the tip in this.

this is usually unnecessary as the plant will root itself quite naturally. Again, the runners can be pegged into pots of compost (soil mix) if you want ready-potted plants.

Division

Raspberries are usually increased by division. It is a simple matter to lift some of the suckers that emerge a little way from the parent plant. In the autumn dig up a healthy, strong-growing sucker and cut through the root that is still attached to the main clump. Replant this in its fruiting position. It is advisable never to divide diseased plants for replanting. If you are in any doubt, it is always better to start from scratch, using certified disease-free stock that has been sold by a reputable nursery.

Methods of Propagation
Division Blackberries, hybrid berries, raspberries and strawberries
Layering Blackberries, hybrid berries and strawberries
Hardwood Cuttings Blackcurrants, gooseberries, grapes, red currants and white currants
Semi-ripe Cuttings Blueberries
Grafting Tree fruits

TAKING HARDWOOD CUTTTINGS

1 Take the hardwood cuttings in the autumn, with each cutting measuring approximately 30cm/12in in length. Cut the cutting off just below a bud.

2 Dig a slit trench by pushing a spade into the ground and levering it backwards and forwards. If the ground is heavier, open the slit a bit more and part fill it with some clean sharp sand.

3 Place the cuttings vertically in the trench at about 15cm (6in) intervals.

4 Dig the spade in a short distance from the trench and lever it so that the slit closes up.

5 Firm down the soil around the cuttings with your foot and generally tidy up the surface of the soil with a rake.

common
problems

Nothing is ever straightforward in the garden – perhaps if it were, many gardeners would give up through sheer boredom. Nature always throws in a few problems just to keep us on our toes. The weather is rarely consistent: it is either too wet or too dry, too hot or too cold. You turn your back for a few moments, and weeds seem to sprout up everywhere. Just when everything looks perfect, plagues of pests and diseases arrive. The gardener has a lot to contend with.

On the other hand, the situation is rarely as bad as many chemical companies would have you believe. Many of the problems are such that you can probably live with them, while others need only minor attention. Chemicals are only usually needed as a last resort.

Weather Problems

We cannot control the weather; we simply have to take what nature throws at us. Nevertheless, there are some ways in which we can limit the worst of its effects.

Wind

Winds can be destructive. Not only can they knock over and break plants, but also wind-rock can cause a plant to move about so that it becomes loose in the soil or it can create a hole around the point at which the plant enters the soil. This fills with stagnant water, and the plant can rot. A dry or hot wind can remove moisture from leaves, making them wilt. Cold winds can create wind-burn, which shrivels leaves. Winds can also make it unpleasant to work in the garden, frequently making the gardener not only uncomfortable but also irritable – not the best of moods to produce a good vegetable garden.

A long catalogue of woes, but the wind can be tamed to a large degree by creating windbreaks of some sort. By far the best defence is a hedge, which filters the wind, cutting down its speed considerably but at the same time not creating turbulence. A wall, on the other hand, stops the wind dead, but it escapes over the top and creates turbulence on the far side, and this can be more destructive than the wind itself. An alternative to a hedge is a form of plastic netting that is designed especially to be used as a windbreak. This is not the most beautiful of materials, but it is extremely functional.

ABOVE **A maximum/minimum thermometer is ideal for keeping track of the temperature both in the open garden and inside a greenhouse.**

BELOW **A hedge provides excellent protection from the wind. It allows some air to filter through, thus reducing the turbulence that occurs with solid features such as walls.**

TOP **Newspaper makes an excellent temporary insulation against sudden frosts in spring. Drop several layers, one on top of the other, to create air pockets. Do not leave on during the day.**

ABOVE **Fleece has a similar function to newspaper. It is very light and will not harm the plants. Unlike newspaper, it can be left on during the day as light penetrates though it.**

RIGHT **If a frost pocket is caused by a thick hedge, stopping cold air rolling down a hill, cut a hole in the base so that the air can pass through and continue down the hill away from the garden.**

Make sure that the poles supporting it are anchored securely because the netting will act as a sail and exert enormous pressure on its supports.

As a rule, a hedge or wind-break netting will create a "wind shadow" of about ten times the height of the barrier. In other words, a hedge 2m/6ft high will create a relatively wind-free area of about 20m/60ft from its base. The degree of protection decreases the further you get from the hedge, and at 20m/60ft from the hedge the decrease in wind speed is minimal.

Turbulence is reduced considerably by the use of double hedges or two rows of windbreak. Set a few yards apart, these give far greater protection than a single barrier.

Frost

There are two aspects to frost. The first is general winter cold; the second is those sudden unseasonable frosts that can wreak havoc among tender, newly put-out plants.

Winter cold is not generally too much of a problem in the vegetable garden because most of the things left in the garden are hardy. In particularly cold areas or in very cold spells, it is a good idea to give protection to some of the permanent crops, such as globe artichokes, by covering them with straw.

There is more of a problem if the garden is a cold one and the soil does not warm up until late in the spring. If your garden is like this, you will find it impossible to start gardening until then, and this makes early crops difficult to grow. There are several things you can do to help, however. If your vegetable garden is in a frost hollow – caused by cold air being trapped within it – it may be possible to "drain" it. Make a hole in the hedge or fence at the lowest point of the garden so that the air can flow through and continue down the slope. Alternatively, hedges may be placed higher up the slope to deflect the cold air as it moves downhill. Covering the soil with black polythene (plastic) or cloches will help warm up and dry out the soil so that you can start work on it earlier.

Sudden frosts can be a nightmare, especially if they are preceded by a warm spell that brings plants into early growth. Keep an ear or eye on the weather forecasts and cover tender plants if frost threatens. Use cloches, fleece or even newspaper.

ABOVE **Some plants, such as globe artichokes, are hardy but can be damaged by severe weather. They can be covered with straw to give them extra protection.**

ABOVE **Filling a box with straw makes a good form of insulation that can be removed and replaced. It also prevents the straw being blown about.**

ABOVE **Cloches produce longer-term protection than straw. They can be used to protect crops through the winter or as temporary cover in spring whenever frosts threaten.**

Drought

Few vegetables and fruit will grow without adequate moisture. Many plants will grow in dry conditions, but they quickly bolt (run to seed) and tend to be tough and often taste bitter. A constant supply of water is necessary so that growth is steady and uninterrupted. Irregular supplies of water will lead to irregular growth and many vegetables and fruit, in particular, will split.

ABOVE **The best way to water a vegetable garden is with a watering can. Water can then be applied to exactly the right spot and in the right quantity with little water being wasted. However, watering by hand is both time-consuming and heavy work.**

Maintaining reserves

Throughout this book there is an emphasis on adding as much organic material as possible to the soil. Once again, this advice has to be repeated. Any free moisture in ordinary soil is likely to drain away or evaporate from the surface. However, fibrous material around the plant's roots will hold moisture in the same way as a cloth or a sponge. If there is excess moisture it will drain away, so that the plant is not standing in stagnant water, but enough will be retained to supply the plant's roots over a considerable time. Even if the water supply depends on irregular rain showers, the slow release will help to mitigate the dry periods.

Working as much organic material as possible into the soil is one way of pre-empting a dry summer. Add it to the soil when it is dug or, if you are using a non-digging, deep-bed system, add it as a top-dressing. Do this every year so that the water-retaining quality of the soil improves.

Keeping water in

One way that moisture is lost from the soil is through evaporation from the surface. Hot sun and drying winds quickly take their toll on the soil and can dry it to a surprising depth, simply because more is drawn upwards to replace what has been lost nearer the surface. Covering the soil with a mulch helps to preserve this moisture.

ABOVE **A dribble hose is a good watering method because the hose is laid along the row of plants and it only waters the immediate area. The water slowly seeps out of the pipe, which means that it does not flood the area, but sinks well into the soil.**

LEFT **Place water butts beneath as many rooves as possible to catch the water as it runs off. It is the purest form of water to use and, being at ambient temperature, it does not chill the plants. It will also save water and, in most gardens, the money spent on water bills.**

RIGHT **Mulching with a layer of grass cuttings helps to preserve the moisture in the soil. Water before mulching and do not use too thick a layer as this may heat up and burn the plant – 7.5cm/3in is sufficient.**

Organic mulches are the best ones to use because they not only act as a barrier, but also eventually break down and are taken into the soil, much to its benefit. A mulch acts as a barrier partly because moisture does not evaporate from it quite as quickly as it does from ordinary soil, and partly because it acts as a thermal barrier, preventing the soil from getting too warm and thus speeding up the drying process.

Non-organic mulches – polythene (plastic), for example – prevent even greater loss as little moisture finds its way through, but, of course, it is not as easy for water to penetrate in the first place. Those to whom the aesthetic qualities of the kitchen garden are important may find that polythene looks ugly and will prefer to use an organic mulch.

It is important that the ground is thoroughly watered before any mulch is applied. If the ground is left dry the mulch will prevent it from getting wet unless a very large quantity of water is supplied.

Watering

Water is an expensive commodity – and becoming increasingly expensive in some areas – so you should use it only where and when it is really needed. Avoid, if possible, using sprinklers that waste large quantities of water on paths and other non-productive ground. If you have the time and strength use a watering can, supplying water to the base of individual plants. If you do this, you can be sure that the water goes where it is most needed. Sprinklers are especially use-ful when there is a large area of produce to cover or if watering by hand is difficult for physical reasons.

One efficient way of supplying water is to use a drip hose. This is a hosepipe (garden hose) with holes in it. It is laid along the line of plants and water constantly dribbles out. There is not enough water to flood the soil, but there is sufficient to provide a constant supply to the plants. If the ground is mulched, lay the pipe under the mulch. These hoses are best left on for several hours until the soil has taken up sufficient moisture, and then turned off, but there are gardens where they can be left on permanently. The system works best with permanent plantings, such as fruit bushes.

Whatever method you use, make certain that the ground is thoroughly soaked. A sprinkling of water on the surface will do little other than lay the dust. To be effective, a watering should supply at least the equivalent of 2.5cm/1in of rain.

LEFT **Black polythene (plastic) mulch is not attractive, but it is effective in reducing the water lost through evaporation. Special horticultural mulch can also be bought which allows water to pass through into the ground but prevents it escaping again.**

Weed Control

Many people are put off gardening simply because they do not like the idea of weeding. However, there are two points that they probably never consider. The first is that in a well-maintained garden there is far less weeding to do than they might think, and, second, weeding can be a rather relaxing, even therapeutic, task.

Keep it clean

Weeds in the right place can be a good thing, but the right place is not the vegetable garden. Weeds take nutrients and moisture from the soil, depriving the vegetables of their share. They can grow tall, smothering or drawing up the vegetables so that they do not grow properly. Many weeds harbour diseases, particularly rusts, and pass these on to your crops. So keep your kitchen garden clear of weeds if you want to produce the best crops.

Good preparation

One way to reduce the amount of weeding is to prepare the ground thoroughly in the first place. If all perennial weeds are removed, either by hand or with weedkillers, the only problem to cope with are new perennial and annual weeds that germinate from seeds. These are not much of a problem as long as they are hoed off soon after they have appeared. If you remove them before they

can run to seed, gradually the number of seeds left in the soil – and hence the number of germinating weeds – will be reduced.

Keeping on top

As long as you keep on top of weeds they are not a problem. It is when you let things slip that it all becomes a chore. Hoe off weed seedlings as they appear and it will only take a few minutes of your time. Allow them to become fully grown and it will take hours to sort things out.

Hoeing

The method of hoeing is often a matter of personal preference. If you have a draw or swan-neck hoe, you scrape the weeds off by drawing the hoe towards you. If you have a plate or Dutch hoe, you push it forwards, slicing off the weeds. If you have a three-pronged cultivator, you pull it through the top layer of soil, disturbing the roots of the weeds. In dry weather a hoe of either kind is

ABOVE **Avoid using chemical weedkillers in the vegetable garden. If necessary, use them to kill persistent weeds when initially preparing the plot. Always follow the instructions on the packet.**

best because you do not want to open the soil too much or water will evaporate. In wetter weather, however, the cultivator can be extremely useful because it opens the soil and allows the water to drain through.

Close work

Weeds do not always conveniently grow between the rows; they also grow in them where it is not as easy to hoe. With well-spaced

BELOW **For delicate hoeing around plants that may be easily damaged, a small one-handed hoe, known as an onion hoe, can be used. It is a form of draw hoe.**

ABOVE **It is not always possible to hoe without damaging the vegetables, or because the weeds are too well advanced. Weeding with a hand fork is then the best alternative.**

TOP **A push, plate or Dutch hoe is pushed forward, slicing either on or just below the surface, cutting off the weeds.**

ABOVE **A cultivator is a form of three-pronged hoe that is drawn between the rows of vegetables. This loosens the earth and with it any seedlings that have just germinated. As their roots are loose in the soil they cannot pick up moisture, and so die. This method is not as good in wet weather because the rain replants the weeds.**

LEFT **Hoeing is the traditional way of keeping a vegetable garden free of weeds. A draw hoe or swan-neck hoe is pulled towards the gardener in a series of chopping movements.**

crops, such as cabbages, it is possible to hoe around them, but this is impossible with vegetables such as carrots, and here you will have to weed by hand. Sometimes there is space to use an onion hoe, a small hoe with a short handle, which is held in one hand.

When you are working close to vegetables be careful not to disturb them. If a vegetable is disturbed when weeding nearby, firm down the soil and water in afterwards.

Non-digging methods

Gardening lore says that one year's weed seed means seven years' hard work, spent removing the resulting seedlings. What actually happens is that the seeds get mixed with the soil and germinate only when they come to the surface – one year's worth of weed seeds, therefore, will continue to be a nuisance until they have all been used up. However, if you do not bring the seeds to the

surface in the first place they cannot germinate, and in non-digging methods only the surface layer is disturbed and the store of weed seeds is quickly used up. In consequence, if you regularly scrape off any weeds that appear, then the amount of work will soon be reduced because the only new weeds will be those blown in on the wind – the rest will be left underground, out of harm's way.

Pests and Diseases

Some gardeners get terribly worried about pests and diseases, but in reality they are rarely a real problem. Common sense and good management mean that you should be able to go for years without feeling the need to reach for the spray gun.

Gardening books always include long lists of pests and diseases and make it look as if these problems are lurking around every corner, just waiting to burst in on your garden and ruin your crops. In fact, it is unlikely that most gardeners will ever see a fraction of these during his or her lifetime, and, if they do, they are probably not really worth worrying about.

A mixed garden

One of the best ways of keeping the garden pest free is to grow a wide range of crops. If you only grow carrots and carrot root fly turns up and devastates your crop, you have nothing left. However, if you grow 20 different types of vegetables, you are only going to lose a twentieth of your total crop, which is relatively insignificant.

A mixed garden, which contains plenty of flowers – particularly the old-fashioned varieties – will attract a host of wildlife such as ladybirds, hoverflies and plenty of other predators, which will attack any pests that arrive in the garden. I have a large cottage garden with several large flower gardens within it and I am rarely troubled by even such common pests as aphids. Indeed, I cannot actually remember the last time any chemicals were used on my garden, not because I am against using chemical treatments, but because it has just not been necessary to do so.

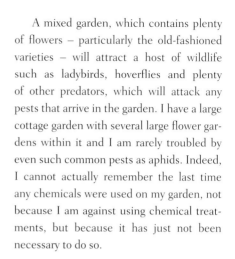

ABOVE **Rabbits can devastate a garden overnight, leaving nothing but chewed off stumps as a result of their visit.**

ABOVE **Birds are one of the worst pests in the garden. Here large bites have been taken out of a brassica.**

LEFT **Nets can be used to guard your crops against rabbits and rodents.**

Animals

There is one type of pest that is very difficult to control – mammals. They can rarely be killed and are difficult to deter. The only real action that you can take is preventative, and this means building a barricade around your garden. Wire netting, which will keep out most animals, should be partially buried in the ground to prevent burrowing species, such as rabbits, getting underneath. For the more athletic species, such as deer, the barrier will need to be at least 2.4m/8ft high if you are to prevent them from jumping over it. Fortunately, there is no need to take action unless you live in an area where these pests are a problem. You will rarely be troubled, for example, if you garden in a town.

Birds

While only relatively few gardeners have deer to contend with, birds are everywhere, and even if things are quiet one day, a large flock of pigeons can appear the next, even in a town. The only real recourse against pigeons is to net everything. A fruit cage that is tall enough to allow the gardener in is the best,

ABOVE **Damage to trees can be prevented by using wire guards.**

RIGHT **Birds and butterflies can be kept at bay with fine-meshed nets.**

ABOVE **Insect damage can cause a wide range of problems. Aphids, like these, not only distort and kill plants by sucking the sap from leaves and stems, but can also introduce diseases.**

ABOVE **The caterpillar stage in the development of butterflies and moths causes a great deal of damage to leaves, especially to members of the cabbage family.**

ABOVE **Mechanical methods are often easier and cause less harm than using chemicals. Here, fleece is used to cover brassicas to prevent butterflies from laying eggs.**

but this is expensive. Low level netting can be used as temporary protection when crops are at their most vulnerable.

Bird scarers are also a possibility, but they are not especially effective. Humming tapes are probably the most effective solution, but they do not always work.

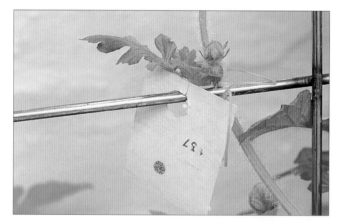

LEFT **Biological controls are an increasingly successful way to fight pests. They are mainly used in greenhouses, but others are now becoming available for the open garden. The control insects are released, here from a sachet, in order to attack the pests.**

LEFT **Sticky traps are another form of non-spray control that is becoming popular for a wide range of pests. Here, pheromones attract insect pests to the trap, where they get stuck. Other sticky traps consist of sheets of yellow plastic covered with a non-drying glue. These are mainly used in greenhouses.**

In addition to eating fruit, buds and leaf vegetables, birds can also cause damage to crops by dust-bathing in the seedbeds of the garden. These can be covered with netting as a deterrent. The birds are usually also deterred if several pea-sticks are laid temporarily on the bed.

Insects

A wide range of insect pests can attack vegetables. Some of these, such as aphids, attack virtually anything; others, such as carrot fly, restrict themselves to one type of crop. Many pests can be deterred by taking simple precautions. Cabbage root fly, for example, can be deterred by placing a piece of roofing felt or plastic on the ground around the plant to prevent the adults from laying their eggs next to the stem. Black fly can be a pest of broad (fava) beans, but if you remove their favourite part of the plant, the succulent tips, before they appear, the blackfly usually do not stop. Small outbreaks of insects can usually be removed by hand before they get out of control.

If the worst comes to the worst, you can use a chemical control. There are types that are safe to use with vegetables, but it is essential to read the instructions on the packaging, especially any advice about safety. Use chemicals only when and where they are needed; do not automatically drench everything. Make sure that spray or powder does not drift onto other plants, especially those that may be ready to be harvested.

Caterpillars

There are three ways of dealing with caterpillars. The first is preventative. Cover the plants with fleece or small-mesh netting so that butterflies and moths cannot lay their

LEFT **Slugs and snails have few friends among gardeners. They make holes in just about any part of a plant, often leaving it useless or even dead.**

eggs. The second is to check susceptible plants regularly and remove any eggs or caterpillars by hand. You may miss a few, but this usually keeps the problem within reasonable bounds. The third is to use chemicals. Again, be certain that they are suitable for vegetables and follow the instructions scrupulously.

Slugs and snails

Mollusc are probably the gardener's worst enemy. There are many traditional ways of ridding the garden of them, including using containers of beer sunk into the beds, but one of the most effective ways is to go out after dark with a torch (flashlight) and round up as many as you can see – and you will be surprised how many you will find. Kill them by putting them in a container of water with added washing-up liquid, or capture and release them on waste ground away from your garden. Doing this for a few nights should help to keep the problem under control.

If you must, you can use slug bait. There are organic baits available if you prefer, but they do not seem to be as effective as the non-organic type. Always follow the manufacturer's instructions to the letter and do not leave either bait or dead slugs around because they may be eaten by wildlife. Biological control is available, but it is expensive, the supply is erratic, and it does not always work; but things should improve on this front.

Diseases

Good housekeeping can prevent many diseases. Remove diseased or rotting material as soon as you see it. Deter aphids,

LEFT **Slugs and snails have few friends among gardeners. They make holes in just about any part of a plant, often leaving it useless or even dead.**

which are often the carriers of disease, and, as a matter of practice, do not use the same ground two years running for the same crop. Wet, ill-drained soil may be the cause of some diseases, so improving the condition of the soil can be an important factor in keeping disease at bay. Healthy, well-fed and watered plants are less likely to fall prey to disease. Never buy, or accept as gifts, diseased plants.

Many modern hybrids are less susceptible to certain diseases than some of the older ones, so choose your varieties with care, if you are worried about possible diseases.

Some diseases can be treated with chemicals, but if there is any doubt, dig up the affected plants and burn them as soon as possible. If you do use chemicals, be careful and follow all instructions, especially the safety ones. Store chemicals well out of the reach of young children.

Burning is the only solution for plants suffering from viral diseases, such as mosaic virus on marrows (zucchini) and cucumbers or on spinach, because there is no known cure. Burning vegetables may seem a waste, but it is far better to safeguard the unaffected plants as well as to prevent spores from getting into the soil. If this does happen, next year's plants might be affected as well. To avoid this, use a rotational system of growing crops.

Remember not to put diseased plants on the compost heap. In theory, the compost should get hot enough to kill off any spores, but you can never be quite certain that all parts of the heap are sufficiently hot, and you might end up spreading the disease over the whole garden.

BELOW **Many of the diseases that affect vegetables are fungal ones, such as this rust on leeks.**

GARDENING CALENDAR

Winter

AW *all winter*   EW *early winter*   MW *midwinter*
LW *late winter*

General
Clean and maintain tools and equipment AW
Plan next year's crops AW
Order seed and plants AW
Order sowing and potting composts (soil mixes) AW
Order manure AW
Continue digging soil when conditions allow AW
Avoid treading or working on waterlogged soil AW
Clean and prepare pots and propagators AW
Compost any organic waste AW

Vegetables
Sow early vegetables under glass for planting
under protection MW–LW
Sow early vegetables for planting out LW
Check stored vegetables AW
Plant rhubarb MW–LW
Sow broad (fava) beans MW–LW
Sow parsnips if conditions allow LW
Plant early potatoes if conditions allow LW
Protect overwintering crops such as peas and broad
(fava) beans with cloches AW
Protect brassicas from birds AW
Force rhubarb LW

Herbs
Continue to remove dead stems from
herbaceous material AW
Continue to prepare ground when
conditions allow AW
Use cloches for protection or to promote
winter growth AW

Fruit
Prune fruit bushes AW
Prune apple and pear trees AW
Heel in bare-rooted trees and bushes when
they arrive AW
Plant bushes and trees when conditions allow AW
Prevent birds stripping buds from fruit bushes AW–LW
Check stored fruit AW
Check supports and ties on supported
trees and bushes AW
Take hardwood cuttings EW

Spring

AS *all spring*   ES *early spring*   MS *mid-spring*
LS *late spring*

General
Prepare seed beds AS
Finish winter digging and ground preparation ES
Keep weeds under control AS
Water in dry weather LS

Vegetables
Mulch permanent beds with manure ES–MS
Begin main sowing and planting of hardy vegetables AS
Continue successional sowings MS–LS
Sow tender vegetables like runner beans under glass LS
Plant tomatoes, aubergines (eggplants), cucumbers and
peppers in heated greenhouses ES–MS
Plant tomatoes, aubergines (eggplants), cucumbers and
peppers in unheated greenhouses MS–LS
Plant Jerusalem artichokes, potatoes and onions ES–MS
Plant permanent crops such as globe artichokes
and asparagus ES
Plant out tender vegetables after last frosts LS
Protect vulnerable new growth from frosts AS
Erect supports for peas and beans MS–LS
Force rhubarb ES
Mulch vegetables LS

Herbs
Finish removing last year's dead growth ES
Sow seed for annuals and perennials ES
Sow tender herbs ready for planting out
after frosts MS–LS
Plant out hardy herbs AS
Prune shrubby herbs ES
Plant out tender herbs after last frosts LS
Take basal cuttings ES–MS
Divide herbaceous herbs ES–MS

Fruit
Mulch bushes and trees with manure ES–MS
Finish winter pruning ES
Remove any winter-damaged branches ES
Finish planting bushes and trees ES
Hand-pollinate early fruit trees ES
Protect blossom from frosts AS
Prune plum trees LS
Thin gooseberries LS
Mulch strawberries with straw LS

Summer

AS *all summer*   ES *early summer*   MS *midsummer*
LS *late summer*

General
Keep weeds under control AS
Water when necessary AS
Keep an eye out for pests and diseases AS
Take soft and semi-ripe cuttings MS–LS

Vegetables
Plant out greenhouse-sown tender vegetables ES
Sow tender vegetables ES
Sow winter crops MS–LS
Continue successional sowings ES–MS
Harvest early vegetables as required AS
Shade and ventilate greenhouse vegetables AS
Dampen greenhouse floor to maintain humidity AS
Pick greenhouse vegetables as they ripen AS
Pinch out side shoots from tomatoes AS
Earth up vegetables that require it AS
Lift and dry onions, shallots and garlic LS

Herbs
Harvest herbs as required AS
Harvest herbs for storing before they flower ES–MS
Plant out tender herbs ES
Deadhead as necessary unless seed is required AS
Cut back herbaceous plant to stimulate
new growth AS

Fruit
Pick early soft fruit ES–MS
Continue to pick soft fruit MS–LS
Pick cherries and early tree fruits MS
Net soft fruit against birds AS
Tie in new growth on cane fruit AS
Summer prune tree fruit AS
Thin tree fruit if necessary ES–MS
Remove spent raspberry canes and tie in
new growth LS
Remove foliage and mulch from spent strawberries LS
Pot up or transplant strawberry runners LS
Tip-layer briar fruit LS

Autumn

AA *all autumn* EA *early autumn* MA *mid-autumn*
LA *late autumn*

General

Continue weeding AA
Compost all waste vegetation AA
Water if necessary EA
Start autumn digging on heavy soils MA–LA
Clean and oil tools before putting away for winter LA

Vegetables

Lift and store potatoes EA–MA
Lift and store root crops in cold areas LA
Remove and compost finished crops AA
Plant garlic LA
Plant spring cabbage EA
Sow broad (fava) beans LA
Sow salad crops under glass EA
Protect globe artichokes, celeriac (celery root) and
celery with straw in cold areas LA
Protect brassicas from birds AA
Check stored vegetables LA

Herbs

Harvest seed as it ripens AA
Tidy away dead material as necessary AA
Protect tender herbs MA–LA
Plant perennial and shrubby herbs AA
Move container herbs under protection MA–LA
Divide herbaceous herbs EA

Fruit

Pick tree fruit as it ripens AA
Store apples and pears AA
Pick late crops of strawberries and raspberries AA
Plant new strawberry beds EA, MA
Remove old fruiting canes from briar fruit and
tie in the new MA
Finish removing old raspberry canes and tying
in the new EA
Take hardwood cuttings LA
Plant new fruit trees and bushes MA–LA
Check stored fruit LA
Check all supports and ties EA–MA

WINTER **It is advisable to protect permanent plants, such as globe artichokes, from winter cold and frost. A straw-filled box is a good source of insulation.**

SPRING **Leeks can be harvested between early autumn and late spring by simply digging them out with a fork. Autumn varieties are not as hardy and should be harvested before midwinter.**

SUMMER **Harvest globe artichokes, in summer, from the second year onwards. Take off the flower-heads before they open and while they are still green, cutting 2.5cm/1in below the head with a sharp knife or secateurs (pruners).**

AUTUMN **Potatoes can be harvested from early summer to autumn, depending on whether they are first earlies, second earlies or maincrop potatoes.**

INDEX